'Hand in hand with the question "what do writers do all day?" is "... and where do they do it?". Katie da Cunha Lewin's book is an intimate delight and radical demystifier, making the conditions, rituals and set-ups required for writing to happen individual, multiple and political.'
Jen Calleja, author of *Fair: The Life-Art of Translation*

'*The Writer's Room* taps into our deep obsession with the spaces associated with creating great works of literature, in the most delightful way ... Da Cunha Lewin takes us on a fascinating historical and personal journey giving us all the permission we need to examine our relationship to creativity and the places from which it is born.'
Penny Wincer, author of *Home Matters*

'Katie da Cunha Lewin takes us on an intriguing journey through time and technology to reveal the public and private worlds of writers, past and present.'
Clare Hunter, author of *Threads of Life*

'Brilliant ... Da Cunha Lewin successfully attempts to unravel that exact mix of solitude and companionship, protection and exposure, silence and conversation that writing requires. A book of rare skill and complexity for all those who love literature and wonder about it.'
Guadalupe Nettel, author of *Still Born*

For my grandmother, the writer

For my parents

like my aunt timmie.

it was her iron,

or one like hers,

that smoothed the sheets

the master poet slept on.

home or hotel, what matters is

he lay himself down on her handiwork

and dreamed.

— Lucille Clifton, from 'study the masters'

Literature is no one's private ground; literature is common ground.

— Virginia Woolf, 'The Leaning Tower'

CONTENTS

Introduction   1

Chapter 1   The Preserved Writer's Room   29
Chapter 2   The Writer's Room in Public   69
Chapter 3   Shared Spaces   109
Chapter 4   Temporary Spaces   149
Chapter 5   Changeable Rooms   187

Acknowledgements   219
Endnotes   221
Bibliography   233
Index   241

William Hogarth, The Distrest Poet, 1740.

INTRODUCTION

I can't say how long it's been there, but I have an image in my mind of the place where writers work. I picture the writer; I picture the space; I conjure an atmosphere of quiet calm in which someone can write for many hours undisturbed. This place contains a desk, on which lie various tools of writing, and perhaps a large window, out of which my writer looks to try to capture the world they depict. There are bookshelves teeming with dog-eared paperbacks, imposing hardbacks, critical anthologies, story collections, art books; my writer is also a reader, and a voracious one at that. They might sit on an old office chair, or one made of wood with a rounded back, but it has a squishy pillow nestled into it to keep the writer comfortable, and a blanket thrown over the arm, ready to keep them warm.

As well as the copious number of books, the writer of my imagination has art on their walls: postcards pinned and askew on a corkboard, prints hung up, and old film posters with a corner that flaps in the breeze. There are other smaller objects too, collected and curated to best inspire, full of meaning and sentiment; the potency of these objects lies in their creative charge – their inherent inspirational potential just waiting to be drawn out through the process of writing. These objects crowd shelves, hang from the door frames, peek out from behind books, or simply sit next to the writer as companions and friends. Sometimes they can become talismans, items of good luck, or part of the ritual of the day, given a pat or a stroke. The writer's room need not be neat, could in fact be the one space of the house where things are supposed to be messy, to show a mind at work. Proper creativity makes for unkempt spaces. Are there crisp packets or orange peel littering the desk? Discarded tissues, unstable piles of books unread, crumpled papers? No writing room can be pristine, but the detritus must not outweigh the buzzing, trembling atmosphere of solemn, serious work.

But what of the person themselves? They are less clear in my mind, a fuzzy outline. What I do know of my imagined writer is that they labour at their work. They are a conduit for that atmosphere they have made, sitting at their desk with a straight back, the pose of the concentrated. They delve into their work, not looking up from the page or the screen for hours at a time. They are a figure

INTRODUCTION

of certainty and of authority; the room tells me that they know what they are trying to make, it needs only for them to catch the creative wisp and fix it down in words.

⌇

This room, with its mystery and romance, was certainly already in my mind when I was a teenager, as I sought to learn about art and writing, and started to read 'important and serious' novels. I wanted to fashion my own creative space, as if, by getting it just so, I would become a writer. Around my teenage desk were pictures from magazines and postcards of art that I understood to be important: I had a portrait of Byron, from 1814, a detail from Leonardo da Vinci's sketch for a painting – *The Virgin and Child with Saint Anne and the Infant Saint John the Baptist* – and a photograph of Virginia Woolf, these little splashes of culture vying for space with pictures of Kate Moss looking chic and brooding images of Orlando Bloom. But at that desk, the only toil and worry I experienced was about completing my history homework on time, and later, the complex sexual politics of MSN.

As the years went on, I began to give a lot of thought to what the writer's room might contain, though there were many aspects that didn't even enter my mind; I didn't imagine this work done on a laptop or a desktop computer; it was always by hand or on a typewriter. I hadn't yet developed the taste for coffee so I gave no thought to the fuel of writing, and couldn't have begun to envision the lengths to which some writers went to create the right circumstances from which creativity might spring. My imagination didn't stretch to the moment of writing itself; in my naivety, I thought writing came from outside of oneself, the ethereal muse to whom so much literature is addressed. I had conjured up this person, anonymous and genderless, huddled over their desk deep in thought, fully legible in their chosen profession, absolutely 'a writer'. The room I had created was infused with something that went beyond my admiration of particular aesthetics, into a realm of mythology. I couldn't picture the moment of writing because I had made the very image of the room stand in for the writer themselves – and by extension the very process of writing. And though the room must be attached to other rooms, other houses and other people, I didn't think about any of them either. It stood outside time, outside the architecture of the house, freed from the everyday. In imagining this untethered space, I was replaying an age-old idea about art and its relationship to the rest of the world, in which the artist is on one side and everything else is on the other. The artist's job, my mythology suggests, is to work across that gulf, understanding the world, and communicating it to those who are waiting for missives from the other side. The writer's room remained always seductive yet timeless, caught in between.

Some of the images we hold of this work of writing originate from the very earliest depictions of it taking place, the lives of monks, and even the lives of those who became saints, sequestered away in the simplest of rooms, working with the inspiration of divine feeling. One of the best known is that of St Jerome, who translated the Bible into Latin, as well as penning extensive commentaries on its contents. The German artist Albrecht Dürer made various engraved versions of it. One example from 1514 has an extraordinary depth of field: Jerome sits at the far end of the space, hunched over a very small writing slope. His desk is bare, except for a small inkpot and crucifix, and he is seriously attending to the work at hand. Dürer's engraving, however, is not all as austere as the desk, and his addition of pillows in differing sizes laid around the room suggests that alongside the concentrated work of the scholar must come rest and relaxation. This is echoed in the detail at the front of scene, with two animals, a companionable pair, asleep. Like many writers, St Jerome is kept company by furry friends. Unlike most, however, one of his companions is a rather diminutive lion, the beast that he is said to have healed by removing a thorn from its paw. In another version from around

1530 by the Flemish painter Pieter Coecke van Aelst, Jerome's desk is equipped with a book rest, on which lies an illuminated version of the Bible, as well as a pair of spectacles, and a candle and knife. But his posture is slumped, and as he holds his brow, one finger rests on the human skull at the very bottom of the image in seeming defeat. Though this seems to indicate that he's following the instructions of the words that sit behind him ('*cogita mori*' or 'think upon death' in Latin), the open book and his forlorn expression seem to communicate another, more familiar feeling: the painful throes of writing exhaustion. Comfortingly, even saints find writing hard.

In my teenage obsession about the writing room, other thoughts began to emerge about what formed a literary life. Could I determine what it would *feel* like to be a writer? Ironically, in wondering about the experiences of writers, I joined a coterie of figures from literature who do the very same thing. Adrian Mole, the self-important teenage diarist from Sue Townsend's *The Secret Diary of Adrian Mole Aged 13 ¾*, wants to invent himself as an intellectual, casually mentioning the great works of literature he is reading (including *Crime and Punishment* and *Madame Bovary*) with the minutest of accompanying reviews. Adrian tries his hand at literature, writing a few poems, before confirming that: 'I have decided to be a poet. My father said that there isn't a suitable career structure for poets and no pensions and other boring things, but I am quite decided'[1] and goes about painting his bedroom in black vinyl paint (obscuring the cheerful faces of Noddy wallpaper) to reflect his new identity. Another teenage protagonist, Anthony Charteris Forster of Patrick Hamilton's *Monday Morning*, is even more obsessed with becoming a writer, indulging in lengthy fantasies about the lifestyle without undertaking any writing whatsoever. For Anthony, the allure lies in an image of hard work done at night while hidden away. Later, when he tries to live out his fantasy, he finds that the actuality is a little trickier:

> After dinner he went to his room, switched on the light, lowered the blind, took off his coat, put on his dressing-gown, lit his pipe, ruffled his hair, got out the small wicker table, put the ink and writing materials on it, adjusted his legs in it, opened at the first page and started thinking, about himself, in a dressing-gown, with a pipe, about to write a novel. The romantically complete novelist.[2]

Anthony's writer is fashioned through his clothing, smoking paraphernalia, and — my favourite detail — the ruffled hair. No writer, Anthony seems to think, should look immaculate, their hair worried repeatedly by anxious hands. He envisions himself as 'the romantically complete novelist' not because of his writing, but because of the pose he is in – even sitting at a table and being in the room seems half the battle. The title of Hamilton's novel references the little bargains Anthony periodically makes with himself, that his life will 'begin' the following Monday, but it also refers to the way he interacts with the idea of creativity itself, something he will be able to channel soon, but not quite yet. For any procrastinator, these kinds of bargains may seem familiar; Anthony's creative spark, his ideas and his talent will arrive – eventually – and given that the book is a semi-biographical account of Hamilton's own life, that longed-for employment of talent is evidenced by the large body of writing Hamilton went on to produce. But in the book, the promise of writing remains only ever that: something that *may* come in a perfect moment in the future. If only, Anthony seems to think, he gets the look perfectly right.

Though Adrian and Anthony are seduced by certain enduring myths about creative life, even for those who have written plenty, the idea of the writing-room scene can still haunt the imagination. Linda Brodkey, a professor of literature who taught writing and composition for many years at the University of Texas in Austin and UC San Diego, describes how she imagines writing to look in strikingly similar terms to my own conjured images: 'When I picture writing, I often see a solitary writer alone in a cold garret working into the small hours of the morning by the thin light of a candle. It seems a curious image to conjure, for I am absent from this scene in which the writer is an Author and the writing is Literature.'[3] I know that for me the image of the writing room has not always been useful for my sense of myself as a writer. Over the years, I have found it hard to occupy the space with confidence, as if I were always about to be found out or replaced by someone who would be able to do the work I attempted with so much more naturalness and grace. Brodkey wonders about this too, and in noting her absence from the scene of writing asks if it is in fact 'not [her] scene at all', borrowed instead from a range of artworks and 'canonical literature'[4] – the descendants of St Jerome's room.

Even so, the image endures. I can't help but be fascinated by the portrayal of writers in fiction, like those in George Gissing's *New Grub Street* or George Orwell's Gordon Comstock from *Keep the Aspidistra Flying*, who suffer at their desks; or I look for the inverse, for those spaces of real writers who have been wildly successful, such as the beautifully cramped shed of Philip Pullman or Toni Morrison's sofa. But perhaps this acquisitiveness is less to do with them and more to do with me, as if I might suddenly become more intellectually or artistically alluring through internalising some particular architecture or layout, allowing me to become one of those people who have never once doubted that they were writers and their work worth reading. Yet though we may culturally come back to that space of the solitary creative, writers and artists themselves have seemed aware that this separateness was always an illusion. The American writer Don DeLillo, over the course of fifty years of writing, often invokes the figure of the writer, a person he describes in his novels and in interview simply as 'the man alone in the room'. His writer figure is partially a way of thinking about himself and his career: he has, to all intents and purposes, been a man alone in a room since he started writing in the 1960s and publishing in earnest in the 1970s. But it is also about the way he conceives of the special kind of solitude on which the labour of writing is based. Nevertheless, though the figure in his novels is isolated, he is never fully severed from everything either. As DeLillo writes in his novel *Mao II*, 'A person sits in a room and thinks a thought and it bleeds out into the world.'[5] There is a relationship between what happens in the writer's room and the world the writer is attempting to understand, even if that relationship feels indistinct and one-way, in this iteration at least. Though we might imagine the writer's room as the most *interior* of spaces, it is undoubtedly looking outwards, towards the world it is trying to represent. A strange dance between public and private.

The British painter, engraver and satirist William Hogarth, who worked in the eighteenth century, was a keen observer of British

INTRODUCTION

society, producing work that depicted many facets of London life, including its seedier, rougher sides. Between 1733 and 1735, he turned his attention to the life of writing, painting *The Distrest Poet*, and later reproducing it as an engraving. The poet in this image sits in a poky garret, at a small desk by a window, but this is not a scene of calm creativity: as he looks vaguely out of the frame his wife sits nearby mending clothing, a cat lies on the floor seemingly undoing her good work with sharp claws, and in the background, nestled in the bed, lies a meaty-looking infant on the verge of a scream. The already-crowded and cramped room is further disturbed by the arrival of a woman demanding payment for a bill, one that, from the looks of the pile of paper on the floor under the desk, is unlikely to be met any time soon. Hogarth later created the engraving *The Enraged Musician*, a companion piece in which a violin player is bothered by the cacophony of people and noise that lies just outside his window, distracting him from rehearsal. These two fascinating (and hilarious) images place both the musician and the poet fully in the centre of the social world. Though the individual may try to separate themself from others, whether in the writer's garret or the musician's room, the outside is always trying to get in.

The idealised version of a writer's room, silent and solemn, arrives as an idea not only through its depictions in art, literature and in the media but also as the very real spaces that are often contained in museums and preserved writers' houses and make up one part of a display about their lives. Literary tourism is a profitable industry and most capital cities have several preserved house museums to lure the bibliophile. An intrepid literary explorer can take a trip to the houses of John Keats, Thomas Hardy, Fernando Pessoa, Jean Cocteau, Emily Dickinson and Louisa May Alcott to name but a few. Though the houses are all very different, depicting different time periods and living styles, an emphasis is often put on maintaining the room in which the writer wrote, recreating it, or presenting a composite version of many different rooms the writer may have worked in throughout their lives. As the academic Nicola J. Watson suggests, literary tourism 'materializes and individualizes reading as remembered experience of place',[6] linking the books we love with the writers who were working in particular houses, settings or rooms. We are reminded, in these spaces, that writing does not just happen, but has to happen *somewhere.*

But what pulls us to the writer's room, to Charles Dickens's study at the Charles Dickens Museum in Holborn, London, for example? Are we looking for evidence of genius in his pen and inkwell, or somewhere behind the blue jug decorated with black olives and green leaves? Or is there something murkier here, the leftovers of words or ideas secreted behind the picture frames or even in the very walls themselves? It can feel almost prurient visiting the famous houses of celebrated artists: at Sigmund Freud's house in Hampstead, his books line the crowded shelves, his collection of antiquities sit in a glass cupboard, and yet Freud himself is not there to mediate or to explain their significance. As I've wandered around a writer's house or museum, I sometimes feel as if I'm trespassing, entering a place where I shouldn't, looking at the objects that make up a life, objects instilled with so much more significance than they can communicate through a quick glance.

These questions leave me wondering how I should be engaging and interacting with these spaces that purport to give a 'true' sense of a writer's creative life. As the academic and biographer Hermione Lee, who has written the lives of Virginia Woolf, Edith Wharton and Willa Cather, suggests it is 'a strong but muddled impulse, a mixture of awe, longing desire for inwardness, and intrusive curiosity'[7] that leads us on these pilgrimages. We may not even be sure ourselves of what we are looking for when we purchase our ticket or plan our route, but I'm fascinated by the impulse. In pursuing writers into their homes, we move beyond simply trying to learn more about them or their work (after all, we have Wikipedia for that) to trickier territories of looking for proximity, even intimacy. Yet I suspect there's even more to our obsession with these places.

A tapestry of desire that *The Writer's Room* will examine and unpick over the coming pages.

Undeniably there is something about *the writer* as a character or an archetype that enthrals us. While writing this book, I have been amazed by how many writers I have come across in popular culture: Hollywood films, from classics such as *Breakfast at Tiffany's* to more contemporary films including *Ruby Sparks*, feature struggling or uninspired writers; the supremely popular works of Irish writer Sally Rooney are about the work and perspective of writers; there are even guides in lifestyle and fashion magazines that instruct us in how to dress like Sylvia Plath. The writer, we understand, is different from others, living a more sensitive, more internal life.

I'm not sure I believe this. My understanding of the writer might be more in agreement with Virginia Woolf, a figure to whom we'll return throughout *The Writer's Room*, who describes the writer not through a focus on their internal life but a clear-eyed examination of the world:

> A writer is a person who sits at a desk and keeps his eye fixed, as intently as he can, upon a certain object – that figure of speech may help to keep us steady on our path if we look at it for a moment. He is an artist who sits with a sheet of paper in front of him trying to copy what he sees.

> What is his object – his model? A writer has to keep his eye upon a model that moves, that changes, upon an object that is not one object but innumerable objects. Two words alone cover all that a writer looks at – they are, human life.[8]

For Woolf, what we must value in our writers are their unique powers of looking and their capability to record what they see. Nevertheless, the writer is always enmeshed in that same material world, anchored to the desk, using a sheet of paper. To be a writer then does not mean to live in some far-flung field of the imagination, but to be in a present moment in a particular place and time. We collect the work our writers publish, hoping perhaps to read everything they produce and thereby gain access into how they view the world, matching our own experiences and desires with theirs. We pore over the minutiae of their lives, where they lived and how they wrote: Marcel Proust in his bed, seemingly surviving only on coffee; screenwriter Dalton Trumbo in his bath, pen in one hand, cigarette in the other; Jane Austen scribbling in small neat handwriting at her little table. And these small details can come to take on such significance. The narrator of Julian Barnes's 1985 novel *Flaubert's Parrot*, Geoffrey Braithwaite, thinks about just this topic. A retired GP, he spends the pages of this tricky novel tracking the life of Flaubert through the traces the writer left behind in his stories, in his letters and drafts, as well as through objects, most obviously in the stuffed parrot of the book's title. This parrot, the apparent model for the bird in Flaubert's story 'A Simple Heart', becomes a way for Braithwaite (and Barnes) to explore his most beloved author: in the course of his travels around France, Braithwaite finds that not one but several 'original' parrots exist, each with its own back story and supposed authenticity. We are left then to wonder how we might ever get close to those we admire from afar or across time – to the 'real' writer – if the things of their existence are also so impermanent.

⌒

Just before my thirtieth birthday I decided to look for a new desk. I have been thinking about writing spaces for some time, and yet I'm still helplessly in love with the image of a desk. I want to be critical, to use my analytical training to examine what lies behind my idealisation and assumptions, but I find myself still day-dreaming and fantasising about the possibilities this new object will bring. I have spent long mornings at weekends looking for this desk, and with it, making promises to myself about better work habits and writing routines. I scour Etsy, eBay, Facebook Marketplace, Gumtree. My search terms are 'painted desk', 'wood desk', 'vintage desk'. I don't want to write 'antique' because I know this is likely to increase the asking price and I am on a budget. I find some old-fashioned leather-topped desks, in various dark woods. They look heavy and forbidding, as if they have been in place forever; they will only ever be a picture, or behind glass somewhere, never in my possession. There are some desks you can purchase that come pre-distressed. The 'shabby chic' desk seems particularly prevalent on Etsy, and often with a higher price tag.

I eventually decide upon a white wooden desk in the Shaker style, found after extensive eBay perusing, bought from a woman who says she can deliver it to my door. On the day of its arrival, she parks around the corner and I watch as she and her husband unload the desk, piece by piece. The three of us walk the few metres to my house, holding a leg or a drawer. As we walk, we chat a little, the husband telling me that their daughter just finished her A levels at this desk. He asks me what I'll be using it for. I decide to say, 'I'm a writer', and I see he's pleased. 'She'll like that', he responds smilingly. I thank them both, say goodbye and begin bringing the pieces to the room at the top of the house. It easily reassembles and soon I am looking at my new object with its drawers to be filled and its surface to be covered with notebooks and tea and candles and mess. I begin to list the new habits that will take place here:

I will be one of those people who gets up very early to write.

I will be one of those people who writes all morning and reads all afternoon.

I will set myself a number of words to be completed every day. I can talk about 'doing my words', and then go outside and play tennis (I don't play tennis).

I will be doggedly tied to my desk, and a deep feeling of calm will descend on me when I sit down to write; I will have made an escape room.

I will be able to spend hours at home, and not sit in bed, or play with my cat, or watch television. This desk will ensure I become serious. It will eradicate my frivolity.

The desk is a serious object to curb my bad habits, a talisman for the future when I will be a better worker, a better writer and, perhaps, a better person.

I start off with aims of keeping the desk very clean, of trying to avoid leaving too much of myself, but this soon proves impossible, mug stains, scrap paper, notebooks, petals and little smatterings of pollen and dust proliferate; the desk was painted white, but through time and use, little bits of its former life are revealed, a fleck at a time: I see that it used to be a baby pink. My cat Bartleby, who loves to sit on my lap and kiss me while I type, leaves her hairs strewn on the surface, in black, ginger and white, as well as little rivers of drool. My life is always present at the desk, though I may try to keep it to the edges.

But this desk will not remain in its place for long. Unlike those of famous writers with their preserved scenes in museums and houses to come, this arrangement is only temporary: my husband and I know this desk can be in this room only until we run out of space. As I arrange my piles of books, proofs, notebooks, pencils and bowls of dried fruits to keep me going, I am aware that everything I'm positioning will alter, that soon there will be a different negotiation of furniture in this room, perhaps a bigger spare bed for a friend who needs to stay because of some life upheaval, or more expansive bookcases for my ever-expanding collection.

What eventuates: a new chest of drawers, a changing mat, a cot. The quiet space of contemplation, of worry, and of work, disrupted by new life. My private sanctuary for writing transforms, bearing the weight of different expectations, and one day, just as the desk came into my home, it will have to have a new owner – there really isn't enough space to keep it here – and my scene of industry will be made anew elsewhere.

Looking around at the things in my room, it's interesting to note the objects I've chosen to make me feel at home in writing: I have a carved wooden elephant in a beautiful dark wood that used to belong to my grandfather, who died when I was young; I have a painting of a woman in a room sitting at a desk reading a book, created and given to me by one of my best friends; I have a converted Victorian gas lamp, one of my prize possessions; and I have an oil diffuser in which I burn palmarosa, sweet orange, lavender and geranium, as a sort of sensory signal to myself to start work. Many of these objects have straddled two writing spaces, carried over from one house to another, rearranged and reorganised. In the moving, I realised that I had a box of objects that had become my writing objects, which would sit with me wherever I was working. They were and are the background against which my writing life has been formed.

So many creatives look to objects as a way of anchoring themselves or centring themselves, or as a way to conjure the words they need into existence. Writer and translator Lauren Elkin keeps a copy of Gustave Caillebotte's painting *The Floor Scrapers* (1875) hanging up nearby as a reminder to work hard;[9] Jen Calleja, also a writer and translator, keeps a little assemblage of contrasting objects, model cottages, worry dolls, a troll in a football kit, even 'a model of a slice of cake I made that I was tempted to get rid of because it was a bit shonky and I rushed the painting on the sprinkles, but I decided I really liked it, so I have it to fight against perfectionism, a reminder that something being perfect doesn't mean it's good'.[10] It feels notable that both writers choose objects that are so contrasting to the work they undertake to root them in this tangible life, even console them in their ordinariness when needed.

Still, inspiring or charged objects aside, it's hard to know where writing comes from or why; sometimes, I am so filled with the desire to sit at my desk and write words, *any words*, until some kind of descent occurs, where I start to feel calm and otherworldly. I've often described the process of writing as plunging underwater; not only is that feeling strange, but the impetus for it even stranger. The writing room helps us envision this lack of presence, as if by situating us in that place, we can begin to give weight to an activity that can otherwise seem mystifying.

During the pandemic we all, in one way or another, spent much more time at home, with many of us trying to find spaces to work in the home for the first time. As we adjusted to our new lives inside, we were purchasing desks, comfier chairs, new plants, and even redecorating or redesigning our homes to allow us to find calm and peaceful places away from our housemates, partners, children or pets. For some, this opened up avenues of possibility about what work could look like, with better work/life balance, less money and time spent on commuting. A few years post-pandemic, as we've seen the variety of benefits of home-based working, a large number of us are resisting going back to the office full time.

Yet even though many more of us found or created spaces to work in our homes during the lockdown, a few years later, getting to use them or keep them is a different story. How do we get to be alone, how and when do we feel able to ask this or demand this from our lives and loved ones? Anyone who has ever written anything knows that it is almost always a solitary act; even if our art is deeply enmeshed in examining or representing the lives of others, we desire the space, whether that's physically or emotionally, in which we can execute our work without disruption. In the writer's room of our collective imagination, it becomes possible for a person to unhitch themselves from their attachments, settling in to the space they have made that not only produces the conditions for work, but helps inspire it. In this dream, the room is a protective bubble, keeping the writer in and the rest of the world out.

Now, years after the purchase of my desk, I find myself newly tethered to the world, more connected than I ever have been, to my son, my husband, my family. Can a writer be enmeshed with others and still do what they want, what they need? Many writers have asked and continue to ask this question as it is not one with a straightforward answer, but I have returned here again and again to Virginia Woolf's famous work from 1929, *A Room of One's Own*. At the opening of the book, the narrator is going to a luncheon at a fictional Cambridge college; the longer she spends in the grounds of the college, the more she begins to think of the money the grounds were built on, and the disparity of achievement between men and women in both academic and intellectual worlds: 'Why was one sex so prosperous and the other so poor? What effect has poverty on fiction? What conditions are necessary for the creation of works of art?'[11] The narrator is then inspired to take a trip to the Round Reading Room at the British Museum in 'pursuit of truth',[12] but she finds that, in the place that purports to give a full account of human knowledge through collecting its literature, women are only ever the subjects of work by men, and seldom the writers of valued work themselves – how we come to measure that value is something I'll be thinking about in the following pages. Woolf concludes that the only way women are ever to breach the gap, to redress that balance somehow and start to write their own literature, is to secure an income of five hundred pounds a year, and find a space to call their own in which they can work and access solitude and privacy. The phrase she uses to illustrate this, of course, 'a room of one's own', one still very much in common parlance today, that writers name as the idealised version of creative solitude. Yet the book is more complex than the phrase would suggest, in that it tied creativity to the practicalities of life, suggesting that creative work does not come from realms otherworldly and unknown but from the realities of finding necessary time and space. Woolf shows that writers are not made solely through their talent, but talent that is allowed and enabled to flourish. She creates the figure of Shakespeare's sister, whom she names Judith, a writer of equal talent to her brother, but who, given her gender and circumstance, dies penniless and unremembered. As Woolf examines the history of English literature, she cannot help but revisit this question of physical space: no matter how and where the writer works, they are always 'attached to grossly material things'.[13] For beyond the notion of the protective bubble, the very practical concerns of the world cannot be set aside.

That connection is vastly complex for many people, sometimes even insurmountable. Women have been told over and over again that creativity is incompatible with having children: the writer and critic Cyril Connolly famously asserted in the 1930s that '[t]here is no more sombre enemy of good art than the pram in the hallway'.[14] Writing this in his work, *Enemies of Promise,* Connolly sought to identify the array of impediments that could stymie potential genius – his own included – conveniently ignoring that, at that time, the 'pram in the hallway' was a given in the lives of most women. For many, time has never felt their own, and so finding moments in which to be creative is to forgo a seemingly inescapable sense of duty to other people. Much Anglophone feminist writing of the mid-twentieth century looked at how the patriarchy curtails the freedoms of women, including their psychological and creative lives. Partly, as Woolf and many other feminist writers suggest, that curtailing is spatial: the refusal to be given space to work or to create tells another story about a refusal to be *allowed* to do those things in the first place.

In writing this book, I didn't set out to try to create a rulebook for writing, nor did I expect to find formulas for how people undertake creative work. Instead, I wanted to find a means of recording just how varied the writing life has been and can be. More than that, I looked for ways that all of us can find to be creative, to ask for things for ourselves *from* ourselves, as well as the people around us.

How many other versions are there of the writer, except the one I imagine in the garret?

The writer with another job
The writer in a queue
The writer who is a carer
The writer who is a mother
The writer who is a father
The writer who is a parent

The writer on a bus

The writer who is not rich

The writer who is not white

The writer who is an immigrant

The writer who is in prison

The writer on the street

The writer with no space of their own

The space of the writing room, though increasingly rarefied, can feel like a credential, an assurance of the quality of the output of the person who works there; the problem of the writer's room is that not everyone has one, or at least, does not have equal access to one. And perhaps, even more importantly, creativity might not always be tied to being solitary. So in this book, we'll explore other writing spaces too: those still based in the home – at the kitchen table, on the sofa, in the living room; those in public where we are surrounded by people, such as libraries and cafes; and those in between, on portable writing desks or typewriters, in hotels, or on the commute. I'd like to create a little more space, open out the writer's room from the four walls, the desk, the chair, the bookcases, the objects that inspire, and find new creative ground. We can let the room stand, for now, but it does not have to be the *only* space that defines the writer and shapes the books we love.

The writing room can tell us a lot about the history of how we have imagined and talked about writers and creativity in the past, but in the pages that follow, we'll also try to build new spaces that can give us a sense of a more accessible future.

Virginia Woolf's writing lodge, Monk's House, Sussex.

Chapter 1

THE PRESERVED WRITER'S ROOM

From the very early days of this book, I knew that my first visit to a writer's house would be the cottage of Virginia and Leonard Woolf. It was a symbolic gesture as much as actual research: after many years of reading and admiring Woolf, I felt it was only right that my first proper trip, on a mild, sunny day in April, would be to Monk's House. Bought by the National Trust in 1981, the house has been preserved so that is looks just as it did when the couple were in residence: vibrant paint on the walls, original furniture, Leonard's favourite flowers filling the garden. Though I have many questions about the mythologising of the writer's space, there is still something incredibly seductive about the idea of actually being in the home of a genius author. And there was a small part that hoped it might spark, if not genius, at least inspiration, for myself.

Woolf's name is so familiar that I've forgotten where I first learned of it, or her work. Perhaps it was the year I received from my parents a collection by Penguin Modern Classics of works that have been adapted into films: Ken Kesey's *One Flew Over the Cuckoo's Nest*, E. M. Forster's *A Room with a View* and Woolf's 1928 book *Orlando*. Woolf's name accompanied me through university. Reading *To the Lighthouse* in the third year of my undergraduate degree, and again during my Masters, Woolf was inscribed into my academic life as someone indispensable, someone who provided ways of understanding what it means to be alive. When in 2014 the National Portrait Gallery hosted an exhibition of Woolf portraits, painted by people such as her sister, Vanessa Bell, and Roger Fry, I attended with Susanna, one of my best friends. As we walked around the gallery, we were surrounded by Woolf's image, often in the pale washes favoured by the Bloomsbury group; my favourites were of her reading or sitting near piles of haphazardly stacked books. I found myself made more curious; I wanted to know what she was reading with such attention, and to peek into her rooms; I wanted other ways to understand how her writing came to be. I bought a print from the gift shop, one of the most well known of her portraits taken by photographer George Charles Beresford, in which she looks impossibly young and elegant. Here she is twenty years old, her long solemn face looking slightly down and out of the frame. I always read it as an image of beginnings, which felt appropriate given my own age then, only a couple of years older than Woolf in the portrait, with serious aims and ambitions, though without direction. This is Woolf while she still had the second name Stephen, her books yet to be written.

On the day of my visit to Monk's House, I felt nervous on the train as I watched the English countryside fly by in smudges of green. I knew I wanted to get something from this trip, but what specifically? I was hoping to find the house beautiful and moving, to feel excited by sharing a space where Woolf had once been, standing on the same bit of floor, or gazing out at the same view. More practically, I wanted the trip to give me ideas, to be full of possible directions to take my writing. And, most embarrassingly, I hoped for some gorgeous Woolf paraphernalia, like a beautiful illustrated image of the house or something simple like a tea towel. I wanted a keepsake, even if it was mass-produced and ultimately unimportant. I had the sense that there was something significant about visiting the home of a person I admired greatly, though it was hard to put my finger on exactly what that was.

Nevertheless I was treading a well-worn path, journeying to a place of note in the hope of finding some trace of one of my most beloved writers. Woolf herself seems to have been aware of the fraught nature of this desire, even in the very earliest days of her career. As she wrote in her first published – though anonymous – piece for the *Guardian*, 'Haworth, November 1904':

> I do not know whether pilgrimages to the shrines of famous men ought not to be condemned as sentimental journeys. It is better to read Carlyle in your own study chair than to visit the sound-proof room and pore over the manuscripts at Chelsea . . . The curiosity is only legitimate when the house of a great writer or the country in which it is set adds something to our understanding of his books.[1]

In this essay, Woolf explores her interest in going to see the parsonage, the home of the Brontë siblings in Haworth, West Yorkshire, partially spurred by her reading of Elizabeth Gaskell's biography of Charlotte, in which both the Brontës' home, and the nearby town of Keighley, provide a backdrop to the lives of the family. Yet it remains unclear why one preserved writer's house may 'add' something to our grasp of a writer's work – thus making a trip there 'legitimate' – while others may not. As Woolf goes on her visit, she finds the town almost ignoring the visitors that are there to look for traces of the sisters (not so today), and out of their uninterest finds some greater sense of authenticity. Without the interest of the locals, Woolf finds that 'our only occupation was to picture the slight figure of Charlotte trotting along the streets in her thin mantle'.[2] Later, when Woolf arrives at the house itself, she is reassured that it is, for the most part, unchanged: what Charlotte and her siblings saw each day, she does too. For the young Woolf, 'legitimate' seems to suggest a past made visible and legible, in which a visitor can think of their writer in their setting unencumbered. On my visit to Monk's House, I found myself looking for the same, a way of visualising Woolf in her home that felt *true*. After taking a cab from Lewes station, I walked down a quiet road, and found a few people milling outside a green gate. These were my literary compatriots, out here for reasons unknown. My dreams of tasteful objects for purchase were quickly dashed when I was greeted with a very simple room in which a National Trust volunteer stood smiling behind the counter; the space had whitewashed brick walls and, charmingly, still gave out old-fashioned tickets, as if I were visiting an old cinema or were taking part in a raffle. There wasn't any Virginia Woolf-themed fragrant soap or notebooks emblazoned with her face, but some titles relating to

Woolf, the gardens of the house and the Bloomsbury group were for sale, alongside a nice collection of second-hand books, very reasonably priced.

I checked in with the volunteer and made my way back to the green wooden gate onto which the name 'Monk's House' is carved. I had arrived at my first house.

⌒

Leonard Woolf noted that '1919 was a great fruit year in Sussex; the trees were laden with plums and pears and apples'.[3] Virginia noticed the same, writing in her diary on 3 July that at Monk's House '[t]here seemed an infinity of fruitbearing trees; unexpected flowers sprouted among the cabbages. There were well kept rows of peas, artichokes, potatoes; and I could fancy a very pleasant walk in the orchard under the apple trees, with the grey extinguisher of the church steeple pointing my boundary.'[4] This glut of produce, and the general fecundity of the gardens, seems to have been one of the many things that drew them to buy the seventeenth-century cottage, purchasing it at auction, before moving in a couple of months later. The care of these grounds was to become Leonard's prime occupation whenever they stayed here. Nestled in a little village called Rodmell, a few miles outside Lewes

THE PRESERVED WRITER'S ROOM

in Sussex, Monk's House was the couple's country retreat, away from their busy social and work lives in London – though even a cursory glance at Virginia's diaries from their many months at the house shows that they were often inundated with guests, including the writers E. M. Forster and T. S. Eliot, as well as Virginia's lover Vita Sackville-West.

The house was a simple building when they bought it, without running water or electricity. Woolf seems to have been charmed by this apparent modesty, finding it 'an unpretending house, long and low, a house of many doors'.[5] She liked the pace and freedom of the life they lived in the country, such a contrast to the intensity of London. The building has kept some of this lightness of feeling all these years later, smallish and airy, its multiple exits and entrances providing the possibility of spontaneity. Though I listened to the words of the volunteers as they told us a little about this place, I walked around the lower floor of the house (the top floor is not open to the public) in a kind of daze, floating from room to room, thinking about the writer who had been there too. I imagined Woolf's voice echoing around the walls, her seated in a chair by the fire, or walking over to the bookshelf and selecting something to read. I couldn't help but notice the decoration: the living room was a very bright mint green, a colour that Woolf herself chose, and filled with objects such as tiles and table tops designed by her sister, the artist Vanessa Bell. Everything here was of characteristic 'Bloomsbury' style – a rejection of stuffy Victorian design, dark colours and foreboding, stolid furniture and instead a celebration of the jumbled, the contrasting and the individual.

Woolf had her own bedroom on the lower ground floor, with a separate entrance and large bright windows. Yet she did not work here for long. Instead, she ventured outside and into an outhouse onto which apples from the tree above would fall with a loud and distracting bang. This outhouse, very low-key in its arrangement and cold in winter, would later be transformed in 1934 to become a proper writing lodge. This was just one of a great number of changes the couple made to the house over several years, gradually altering the layout of the rooms and adding a bath and an oven as their fortunes improved, thanks to the increasing popularity of Virginia's work and Leonard's attentive book-keeping. For the scholar Victoria Rosner, Woolf's move from her room to the shed was important in not only the way it allowed her to claim her own space – after all so much of their income came from her work that she had clearly earned the right – but also as a way for her to signal her removal from the household: 'writing outside the house was a way to isolate herself from interruption'.[6] Or, as the British writer Jeanette Winterson neatly describes, it was a kind of 'divorce from domesticity';[7] Woolf's journey elsewhere, even only a few metres, allowed her an important psychological distance from the rules of home.

After Woolf's death, the writing lodge was extended to become a larger studio for Leonard's new partner, Trekkie Ritchie Parsons, an artist. Today, half the room stands behind glass while the other half is open, displaying various photographs of the individuals that visited Leonard and Virginia during their time at Monk's House. Woolf's writing desk sits behind the transparent pane, recreated as a messy scene of writerly industry, with crumpled paper, a vase filled with daffodils, and various covers of her books, again designed and painted by Vanessa (who did so many of the covers for their Hogarth Press), strewn across the desk's surface. The contrast between the apparent haphazardness of the desk and the polished glass makes the scene feel oddly stilted, almost *too* composed, as if we look at a curiosity in a zoo. Jeanette Winterson wrote of her trip to Monk's House and also found this set up strangely alienating, calling it 'the most disappointing room [that] yields nothing of the atmosphere of [Woolf's] writing life'.[8] As Woolf did with the Brontë siblings, so Winterson looks for legitimacy and authenticity in the home of the writer she so admires. But in the staginess of the scene, she feels only the lack of Woolf: 'she is long gone. The sense of someone else having taken over the space is all too pervasive. Here is the writer behind glass, mummified, invented.'[9] I didn't feel that sense of disappointment quite as strongly as Winterson, but there was certainly something strangely lifeless about Woolf's shed. Maybe what Winterson describes is not only the experience of *this* room for her, but all preserved writer's rooms, in which the experience is always to know that what we see is, in reality, a fiction.

In spite of these feelings, and the noticeable absence at the centre of the scene, I took a picture on my ancient iPhone. On the train on my way home, I studied the photo; it was unavoidably bad, slightly out of focus and obscured by the glare from the glass that no amount of angling my hand could avoid. Nonetheless, I didn't delete it; it felt somehow that I had a piece of Monk's House as long as the image stayed on my device. I'll find myself, over the course of the months in which I'm writing this book, checking and re-checking it. Even in the knowledge that the room had not been quite what I wanted, I still took a snapshot as a souvenir, in the hope it would allow me some of its magic.

Part of this sense of otherworldliness is in the presentation of the scene itself, the authoritative locus point for Woolf's creativity. Yet it was only ever one of a number of places where Woolf wrote. She was not necessarily always at the desk and instead, as Leonard writes in his autobiography, was often to be found sitting in a low chair with a much more makeshift set up:

on her knees was a large board made of plywood which had an inkstand glued to it and on the board was a large quarto notebook of plain paper which she had bound up for her and covered herself in (usually) some gaily-covered paper. The first draft of all her novels was written in one of these notebooks with a pen and ink in the mornings.[10]

This casual arrangement is familiar to me; I am always trying to ignore the seductions of writing in comfy spaces, like an armchair, or more likely nestled in my bed. I wonder why, if Woolf's proclivity is a well-documented fact, the lap board and chair is not part of the display? When I spoke to Alli Pritchard, the manager of Monk's House, she explained that as they did not have either any more, they did not want to make something up, as 'visitors (generally speaking) do not like us to present "fake" things'.[11] But I also wondered if curators had to be led by the expectation from a curious audience to *see* a desk; after all, Woolf is the writer of an entire text that considers the importance of a room of one's own. Visitors want to see this borne out. Academic Nicola Watson suggests that the constructed image became increasingly important in a writer's house once photography became much more readily available, and authors could be photographed in their own spaces: '[i]t became necessary as a novelist to be depicted working at a desk, whether you actually did so or not'.[12] Agatha Christie, writer of over sixty novels, was only too aware of this idea: 'I never had a definite place which was *my* room or where I retired specially to write.'[13] Yet journalists, Christie found, were always very keen to place her at a desk and capture her in (apparent) full flow, though she was rather more flexible in the way she worked than they (and likely their audiences) wanted her to be, 'All I needed was a steady table and a typewriter.'[14]

    Leonard's descriptions of his wife's work illustrate not only the impossibility of defining decisively 'where' writing takes place, but also how it is affected by the interplay between place and person, and particularly between home and person. Woolf's routes through her home, perhaps to get another cup of tea, or on the way to the bathroom, are not and cannot be recorded, and yet we know that she would have done these and so many other actions like it hundreds of times. While not all writers' houses are the same in their approaches to preservation and display, they all nonetheless endeavour to show that not only did the writer work in these preserved spaces, but that they dwelled there too. Their personal and their work lives intermingle through the arrangement of objects, the recreations of scenes, or the narratives these curators give each room of the house. Edith Wharton, for example, designed both the house and the grounds of the home she moved into in 1902, The Mount in Massachusetts. The curators there have chosen to replicate the original interior, with much time and attention spent in returning some of Wharton's actual books from her extensive collection back to this space, so that her library here could be repopulated with those tomes that meant so much to her. At the Honoré de Balzac House in Paris, two pages from the esteemed writer's 1842 novel *La Comédie humaine* are neatly laid in parallel on his walnut writing table, as if waiting to be hand-corrected by the author in ink and pen. These preserved spaces are more than the desk, fleshed out through the possible narratives suggested by a writer's personal effects. Here we are reminded that the rooms we now stand in used to be inhabited by the bodies of the writers we have sought to visit, that the works we read were thought up, written and edited by someone *real*.

Drafts, manuscripts teetering on a desk, books and pens askew, are all used as a way of trying to get people to sense, I think, all the things that are *not* preserved in a writer's house museum. The preserved spaces we move through are nearly always conspicuously clean, a contrast to the inevitable mess of living creativity. Leonard, for example, describes Virginia as an untidy writer, an accumulator of what Lytton Strachey termed 'filth packets', which were made up of 'old nibs, bits of string, used matches, rusty paper-clips, crumpled envelopes, broken cigarette-holders, etc'.[15] The scene that he describes cannot be translated to the present; curators instead rely on gesturing towards work or ways of living that we can't find in a room that is carefully maintained and staged. After all, as Leonard writes of Virginia: 'unlike most people, she was almost always at her work even when she was not working'.[16] There is no beginning and end of writing work: the 'scene' of writing is everywhere.

How do we understand the tension between domestic demands and the reality of writerly labour in these preserved spaces? The answer is never clear-cut, particularly in the case of writing by women. The American poet Emily Dickinson is often considered in relation to the space of home, given that she never moved away from her family, and towards the end of her life never physically left its boundaries. In a letter from 1869 to author and abolitionist Thomas Wentworth Higginson, to whom Dickinson would talk about writing and send poems, she explained, 'You noticed my dwelling alone. To an emigrant, country is idle except it be his own. You speak kindly of seeing me; could it please your convenience to come so far as Amherst, I should be very glad, but I do not cross my father's ground to any house or town.'[17] From her letters and her behaviour, many critics have suggested it is likely she was agoraphobic, and that her relationship to her home was determined by her confinement within it. But, for me, it seems more complex than simply the site of a long and painful captivity; Dickinson's writing emerged from the house she lived in, the place in which she was with her family and with servants, in which she laughed, and talked, and baked cakes. The location, the dynamics between herself and other people, as well as the very sense of home itself, became a part of her writing process, a process, we learn through her drafts, that did not necessarily take place in one part of the house, or indeed in one manner; many of Dickinson's poems are written on the edges of letters, the backs of envelopes, or even on recipes. Dickinson's writing was happenstance, a moving and living thing that found its home on the day-to-day scraps of life.

The Emily Dickinson Museum in Amherst, Massachusetts, established in 2003, comprises two houses: the Homestead, which was her home, and the neighbouring Evergreens, where her brother and his family lived. I visit this preserved house virtually several times, watching the videos of the parlour, the library, and Dickinson's bedroom. In this version, the rooms are completely empty, no visitors or guides, making the act of looking around the home even more voyeuristic: I am strangely alone on my sojourns. Dickinson's bedroom is light and airy, a cream wallpaper decorated with pale-pink roses providing the backdrop to the simple furniture. Just off centre is a stark white cotton dress on a dressmaker's dummy. The dress is, in many ways, unremarkable, made in a common design of the time, with a neat, rounded collar, long sleeves, and buttons that run about three quarters of the way down; it is the kind of dress that many women in the nineteenth century would have worn indoors. However, as the poet Mary Ruefle notices, the dress contains potential clues about its wearer, for an outside pocket, 'completely outside, a workman's pocket', has been added, 'level with the sleeve of the right hand. And no curator, no costume historian, can come up with a reason for that pocket to be there, if not to hold something the wearer used with regularity and wanted to be always near – could it have been something to write with, and a piece of paper?'[18] Ruefle sees the dress not just as evidence of the woman who lived in the home, but the writer who worked there: it is not just a pocket but a 'workman's pocket'. The dress, encasing the stand-in mannequin beneath it, encourages visitors to imagine the body that once moved inside it, as if it is Dickinson who is welcoming us into her bedroom and guiding us towards the little writing table nestled near the window. Unlike those in the houses of Balzac and Dickens, this table is not grand, nor situated among objects: instead it sits quietly and unassumedly, much like the writer herself.

THE PRESERVED WRITER'S ROOM

There is, as this book attests, an undeniably romantic and alluring quality to the desk space – and all the potential it encapsulates. This feeling is perhaps made more intense when we know that the person who sat at it wrote significant and immensely influential works, the reach of which is still felt today. This is clearly true in the case of the founder of psychoanalysis, Sigmund Freud, whose ideas about the human mind shaped the twentieth century and informed the practice of literary and critical theory.

Freud's desk sits in his study at the Freud Museum in Hampstead, a room painstakingly recreated from its original home at Berggasse 19 in the city of Vienna. I had been to the Freud Museum many times before, but on this particular visit, on a humid August day, I was surprised to see quite how many people were in attendance. Tourists, locals and even some small children milled about, looking at the displays and walking around the shady, well-maintained garden. I headed straight to the large downstairs room, Freud's study, in which we discover his original couch covered in thick Turkish carpet and patterned cushions. One of Freud's patients, Sergei Pankejeff, known as The Wolf Man because of his famous childhood nightmare, wrote of the original treatment space in Austria that 'The rooms themselves must have been a surprise to any patient, for they in no way reminded one of a doctor's office . . . Everything here contributed to one's feeling of leaving the haste of modern life behind, of being sheltered from one's daily cares.'[19] The room still holds this feeling, appearing much more like a place of quiet contemplation and reflection than diagnosis. Though the couch looms large in the mind of anyone who has read any psycho-analysis, it does in fact feel rather diminutive, sat neatly next to the wall. What the eye is caught by instead is the sheer abundance of paintings, sculpture and antiquities that fill every surface and wall. Freud collected small figures, totems and other miscellaneous objects over the course of many years and kept them around his treatment room, a fascinating mish-mash from different time periods and countries, an enormous crowd of humans, gods and animals, keeping Freud company as he laboured – while he was deep in thought, he would even stroke the head of the little statue of the Egyptian baboon god Thoth that sat on his desk. The desk, as it is now, its layout meticulously copied and recreated from images and diagrams, feels much more like a shrine to the writer, rather than connected with the act of writing itself.

Though the museum includes information about the escape from Vienna, it struggles to give a sense of just how close Freud and his family came to a horrendous end. This quiet street in Hampstead, with its orderly uniform houses and green gardens, feels very far away from the horrors of the Holocaust, though it must have been a scene of such grief and sorrow; indeed, all of Freud's sisters would eventually be killed by the Nazis, either dying in gas chambers or in ghettos. As Hitler gained increasing power in the 1930s, so the Freud family's life in Vienna became more precarious, psychoanalysis targeted as a 'Jewish science'. Not long after Hitler gained a majority in the Reichstag in Germany in 1933, all of Freud's published books were destroyed as part of a mass burning of materials created by Jewish intellectuals and writers, and anything else deemed 'un-German'. The modernist poet Hilda Doolittle, known as H.D., undertook two series of sessions with Freud – one in his home in Vienna between 1933 and 1934, and later when visiting him several times in London. On one of her earlier appointments, she notes the encroachment of the Nazis into the Freuds' home, seeing a path of swastikas immediately outside his building: 'They were chalk ones now; I followed them down Berggasse as if they had been chalked on the pavement especially for my benefit. They led to the Professor's door – maybe, they passed on down another street to another but I did not look further. No one brushed these swastikas out. It is not so easy to scrub death-head chalkmarks from a pavement.'[20]

After Austria was annexed in 1938, the danger became all the more real, with Freud's daughter Anna narrowly escaping transportation after lengthy interrogation from the Gestapo. Many of Freud's supporters and friends rallied together to help the family flee to London. French writer and analyst Princess Marie Bonaparte, who had been a patient of Freud's and a later champion of the work of psychoanalysis, was crucial to the escape, her funding and efforts helping the family gain the necessary visas. But what of the study in which Freud's transformative works had been conceived and produced? In the days leading up the family's departure, Freud's friend, the psychoanalyst August Aichhorn, asked photographer Edmund Engelman to take a photographic inventory of the apartment, in order to ensure that the treatment room and study could be recreated later when Freud's belongings followed the family to England. Engelman agreed, in the knowledge that his work would have to be done discreetly: 'Flash and floodlights were out of the question. I had been told that the apartment was under constant surveillance by the Gestapo.' Over the next few days, he sought to take as many images as possible in order to create the 'only permanent record of the place where Freud had lived and worked for the last forty years ... without arousing any suspicion whatsoever'.[21]

In early June 1938, the Freud family arrived in London, moving into 20 Maresfield Gardens shortly after, where the Freud Museum stands today. The building, an attractive Queen Anne

THE PRESERVED WRITER'S ROOM

style red-brick house, had very different dimensions from that of the apartment in Vienna, so the family had to rearrange the way they lived. Nonetheless, between them and their housekeeper Paula Fichtl, who had travelled with them, Freud's study was reborn. Each item had miraculously made the journey, and his prized collection of antiquities was placed in the same glass cabinets that had housed them previously. Sadly, Freud was to live for only a short time, dying in September 1939 after a long struggle with his painful cancer of the jaw. In his last days, his bed (which was actually another kind of couch, this time one specially made for the ill and disabled) was placed in the study, so that he might look out into the garden. Unlike any other place I visited in person, this preserved writer's room was also the room in which the writer had died.

On the trip here in August, I bought a print of the desk, on which many figures stand sentinel, surrounding a pile of papers, and next to them, half folded, a pair of lightweight rounded spectacles. My purchase was not merely as a decorative object; I wanted to remember the space not only as the place it is today, but to have a reminder of where each object had been before, each of them an anchor, or a portal through time. This room is the site of a near miss, and a testament to the people around Freud who were determined for him and his work to find a place of safety, and for his famous room to endure. The objects we see and their placement in the room tell a story not only of Freud's idiosyncratic writing scene, accompanied by so many items from antiquity, but also of the act of preservation, for us as future visitors but also for Freud himself. Though Freud lived only a few months in England, he continued to use the room in much the same way he had in Austria, as a place to see and treat patients, as well as to write. In Freud's participation in the recreation of his room, there is an acknowledgement of the importance of space in his work, that the room was in fact a necessity for its continuation, however long that would be.

There are other writing rooms that have seen the collaboration of many people in order to ensure their preservation. On another summer's day, I made my way down a quiet residential street not far from South Kensington station, admiring the white terraced houses and the full window boxes. Like Hampstead, this is an area rich with cultural history: in the short distance it takes me to reach my destination, I walk past a blue plaque commemorating the Hungarian composer Béla Bartók's short stay in one house, and another marking the British director Carol Reed's residence. The closer I get to the Thames, the older the houses become. I'd only ever passed Cheyne Walk on the way out of London, on the hot and cramped coach my husband and I would take to Cheltenham to go to visit his parents. Blue plaques would whiz by — or sometimes

I'd have ample time to ponder them if we were stuck in traffic – George Eliot, Dante Gabriel Rossetti, Mick Jagger.

My destination was the slightly less showy Cheyne Row, a much shorter street that sits perpendicular to the river, to visit the house of Thomas and Jane Carlyle, who moved into the house in 1834 and lived there until their deaths, Jane in 1866 and Thomas in 1881. As well as the writer of many important books on the Victorian bookshelf, Thomas also helped establish the London Library, first as part of the original board and later as president from 1870. He was deeply entrenched within the cultural circle of the era, and his house in Cheyne Row was visited by many, including Charles Darwin, Charles Dickens, Robert Browning and Henry James. Jane Carlyle, though not a well-known writer, was widely admired for her wit. American critic Elizabeth Hardwick writes that her 'letters, published after her death, are more brilliant, lively, and enduring than all except the best novels of the period'.[22]

Because of Carlyle's centrality in the literary and cultural world, after he died in 1881 it was quickly realised by his contemporaries and fans that his house must be preserved for the future. A publication from 1896, *Carlyle's House Catalogue*, produced the year after the Carlyle's House Memorial Trust was established in 1895, contains an essay by the Manchester businessman George A. Lumsden, whose extensive efforts helped found the trust and turn the building into the very first writer's house museum in London. He explains that a couple of years previously he had wanted to visit Carlyle's House since 'one of England's greatest men had lived and worked in it, the man whose influence upon my own life had been, in many important respects, determinative',[23] but had found on his arrival, on 8 April 1894, that '[a]ll was dingy and dirty, the windows particularly manifesting those signs which one usually associates with an empty, neglected house'.[24] After this discovery Lumsden springs into action, trying to contact anyone who might know about the house's status. He ascertains that the proprietor is looking to sell, and so he, along with his friend Alfred Miller, sets about trying to convince others to buy into a collective purchase. His account is very touching, detailing his trials and tribulations, his despair, and his desperate need to save the house from an ill fate – a narrative that is interestingly replayed across many writer's houses I've visited or read about, as if in some sense the writer too is also 'saved', or perhaps their life extended. Eventually a committee is formed and on 19 December 1894, nineteen men meet, including the writer and founder of the Dictionary of National Biography Sir Leslie Stephen, Virginia Woolf's father, who is made chairman. After much fundraising, the house is bought, refurbished and opened to the public in July 1896.

The strength of feeling that Lumsden demonstrates shows that for him and the others involved in the establishing of the trust, the need to preserve was a way of recognising the importance of the writer. As with Freud's house, Carlyle's contemporaries and friends agreed that arrangements of the living space had to be recorded for the future – even before he died. The illustrator and painter Helen Allingham and the photographer and good friend of Carlyle, Robert Tait, had the foresight to document the interiors: Tait in photography, and Allingham in pencil sketches. Lumsden notes that both sources were later used in the refurbishment and decoration of the house, aiming to restore it to how it looked when the Carlyles lived there, down to the placement of the picture frames.[25]

The study that we see there today is set up with dark-wood furniture, a large patterned carpet in blues and oranges, portraits on the walls of the topics of his writing, preserved as a place of quiet industry to communicate Carlyle's studiousness, his seriousness. In contrast to those aspects of the room that are supposed to feel 'living' are the exhibits behind glass – open books, letters – offering visitors evidence of the activity that went on in here. But there is much the room can't convey and, in reality, this attic study was a site of much struggle for the couple, proving to be, as Carlyle himself put it, a 'failure'. The writer had become increasingly affected by noise, by bad sleep and, at one point, by a neighbour's energetic rooster; he even wrote to the neighbour asking if it could be 'render[ed] inaudible from midnight to breakfast time . . . as an act of good neighbourship'.[26] But in spite of the silenced bird, Carlyle was soon overwhelmed by other street noises, including irritatingly an increasing number of *other* chickens. The decision was made in 1853 that he needed a 'soundproof' room at the top of the house from which he could write, finally undisturbed. The house had already undergone substantial improvements by this point, with water pipes added and rooms newly papered, but this final project was to be the most complex, costly and, in the end, unsuccessful: the design of the room, which was supposed to ensure its protection from voluble street noise with additional internal walls, did not work; 'I fear . . . that "quiet" is far off me yet,' Carlyle said, while Jane commented, 'The silent room is the noisiest in the house.'[27]

Though there was clearly much interest in maintaining their house in the late nineteenth century, today Carlyle is not as central a figure as he once was. My visit, truthfully, was motivated by a piece I had read by Virginia Woolf. As a daughter of Leslie Stephen, as well as a child of the Victorian age, Woolf was well aware of Carlyle. She had mentioned him in her first published piece on the Brontës' home, and the title of the essay she wrote on visiting his museum home, 'Great Men's Houses', has the sense of being in conversation with Carlyle's own work, *On Heroes*, in which he discusses various 'heroic men', who include poets and men of letters. Written as part of a series of six essays for *Good Housekeeping Magazine* published between 1931 and 1932, Woolf considers how we feel when entering places where writers, the 'Great Men' her title suggests, have lived. She finds that 'we know them from their houses' and yet there is something very particular for her in the way that 'it would seem to be a fact that writers stamp themselves upon their possessions more indelibly than other people'.[28] For her, these men seem 'to possess a much rarer and more interesting gift' than artistic flair, 'a faculty for housing themselves appropriately, for making the table, the chair, the curtain, the carpet into their own image'.[29] The writer's house is more than the walls that make it up, it is everything that it contains too, objects selected that seem to speak in the voice of the writer, even when they are not there. When visitors go to see the preserved rooms of their favourite writers, they aren't only getting a sense of the writer in that specific place, they are using the composition of that space as an imaginative way to trace the emergence of the writer's ideas, or even the way that person may have fashioned themselves as that specific type of being – 'the writer' – in their own eyes, or the eyes of others. By putting themselves in the same position as the writer, perhaps by looking at the same wall, or out of the same window, or even adopting the same position in the chair, visitors may hope to understand the route of creativity.

There also seems to be (as there often is in her writing) a touch of irony in Woolf's voice, as she points out is that it is the act of *preservation* itself that makes the possessions of a writer appear so much more valuable. Which writer's rooms we choose to preserve (and those we don't, as we'll explore in our final chapter) tell us a lot about our cultural and literary inheritance, not only the texts that make it up, but also where and how it was produced, by whom and, crucially, how we might want to remember it. But in this preservation, there is much left out, much that is missing and much more that is obscured. Woolf is sensitive to this in her writing on the Carlyles; as she continues to reflect on the uniqueness of their home, she dwells not on the writer, but on the upkeep and the maintenance of the house itself, undertaken by Jane and a changing roster of servants. 'All through the mid-Victorian age the house was necessarily a battlefield where daily, summer and winter, mistress and maid fought against dirt and cold for cleanliness and warmth,'[30] Woolf writes. Rather than emphasise Carlyle's wrestling with words – and he apparently hated writing – she looks to the unseen work of the female residents: 'The voice of the house – and all houses have voices – is the voice of pumping and scrubbing, of coughing and groaning.'[31] Woolf is listening out for the women whose endeavours enabled Carlyle to do the writing that led to the very preservation of the space in the first place. She conceives of this place as 'the scene of labour, effort and perpetual struggle', not only in the intellectual and creative realm, but so too in the physical. Behind every writing space there may be many others who work hard to allow it to exist at all.

⌒

The hidden labour that allows the writing room to come into being – and to remain – is various in its many acts of creation and indeed preservation. When thinking about a preserved writer's room, we might think first and foremost of curators, archivists, historians and literary academics, but there are also the caretakers, cleaners, restorers. The former might produce the intellectual environment of the museum itself, but the latter *maintain* that space and are as much a part of its creation. On my first visit to the Dickens Museum in Holborn, I spoke with one of the guides there several minutes, at first asking questions about the collection items and the life of Dickens (unsurprisingly, I was rather focused on the desk), but after a while, other things – including why she was there at all. She seemed pleased to be asked, and said it was her admiration for Dickens as a writer, and also a campaigner. This appreciation was borne out in her knowledge: she recounted anecdotes about his time in the local area, the streets around King's Cross, the night walks he would undertake when he was unable to sleep, and the way they changed his views of London. Her presence enlivened the room, providing another way of narrating the story of the objects that surrounded us – not of the genius author, but of the sensitive and interested reader. At the Carlyle House, the two volunteers I spoke with, again older and retired, were not so much fans, but were instead interested in the idea of history and preservation. They proved to be strikingly busy, running up and down the stairs, answering the door, putting people's bags away, and generally seeing to the smooth running of the house, in a way that felt not unlike Jane Carlyle or one of their servants. When I asked the manager of Monk's House, Alli Pritchard, about what the work of preservation involved for her, I was astonished at the detail of her answers:

> Mowing and weeding, deadheading, propagating, sowing seeds, raking leaves, cutting hedges and trees, clearing gutters, sweeping paths clear of mud and leaves, sweeping conservatory, watering conservatory pots and garden beds when required, cleaning windows, washing down woodwork (everything is painted at MH), vacuuming floors,

waxing floors, dusting, dusting for cobwebs, repainting walls when required, checking pest traps and relative humidity monitors, condition checking of items in the collection, inventory checks, updating online collection catalogue, remedial work to collection, putting house to bed in winter and reopening in spring with full cleans. Pretty much the only things we do differently to a hundred years ago is lay a fire and hoovering.[32]

Where Woolf envisioned the voice of the Carlyle House as the guttural sounds of physical labour, so we see that often the work of 'preserving' a house entails much the same care as living in one.

At other places I visited, there were no volunteers forthcoming. At Keats House in Hampstead a slightly disinterested teenager sat at the front desk that also served as a counter from where a visitor could purchase various Keats-related memorabilia – a lot of quotes from his most famous poems on fridge magnets or mugs. In the surrounding garden, a group of cheerful older people gathered eating biscuits and drinking tea, getting ready to see to the bushes and plants that were all looking a bit parched after some hot weather. But I missed having people in the house, guiding me through, and telling me about their particular version of the writer who lived there.

Truth be told, I had much less interest in visiting Keats House than I did many other places, my ambivalence stemming from knowing that Keats lived in the house only for less than two years between 1818 and 1820. I couldn't help but feel, unlike other houses where the writer *must* have left some sort of mark, 'stamped' as Woolf would have it, that it was unlikely that Keats had managed to leave any sort of impression here at all. And in fact, this was true in the sense that in contrast to most of the other museums I visited, Keats House has been substantially altered, by a tenant who closely followed after the poet's departure. The actress Eliza Jane Chester had knocked down the walls that divided what was once two separate houses into one, as well as adding an extension. Though I could walk into the wine cellar and imagine Keats doing the same, the majority of the house would not have been familiar to him. There were few objects or bits of original furniture in situ, and even in the room designated as 'Keats's Parlour', the desk that was supposed to indicate his space of writing had on it an inkwell that belonged to his contemporary Percy Bysshe Shelley. The scene seemed to collapse under all these absences, the mirage of the writer's room destroyed. I knew those two objects had never actually 'lived' together in the times that either poet was writing, and that Keats had never sat at this desk. As if to act as a replacement for these

THE PRESERVED WRITER'S ROOM

missing objects, a soundscape of papers rustling and a teacup being stirred by a spoon played softly from a speaker in the corner of the room, attempting to capture the feel of the act of writing by other means.

The Keats House did have a strange feature that I found myself drawn to, however. It was a copy of Keats's life mask, rendered in what seemed like plastic and painted silver, accompanied by instructions that insisted that we should 'please touch'. Though this is clearly meant to get children involved in the exhibit, and perhaps for those who are visually impaired, I found myself also wanting to touch it, to do as the instructions told me. I stared closely at his face, noticing the shape of his lips, looking for signs of vitality in the way it was composed – this, after all, was his 'life' mask and, therefore, should contain a sign of his life. I decided I would run my fingers across his cheeks and stroke the brows, feeling very self-conscious and strange as I did so. At the same time, there was a power to this intimacy, a reminder that this person had lived. That this person had been a body with a face, a mind. I felt less connected to Keats the writer than to Keats the man, occupying this same space 200 years ago.

The strange feelings of disappointment that I had towards the Keats House experience demonstrates that, though I tried to curb it in myself, I too was looking for some idea of authenticity in the houses I visited. I wanted objects and furniture and belongings displayed in a way that felt *real*, verifiable even. Yet of course, for Keats, this was always going to be a tall order, since he died young and without much money. It wasn't possible for him to leave an extensive collection behind because he didn't have it in the first place, and this house had only ever been a temporary residence.

Where is the limitation to this idea or desire for authenticity? How far do we want our curators to go? Roald Dahl's famous writing shed was moved from the garden of his home to the Roald Dahl Museum and Story Centre in 2012. The move – which wasn't without controversy after the Dahl family asked the public to fund the £500,000 costs to transport and restore this writing space – saw the complete dismantling and recreation of the building inside the museum itself. Though, as we've seen, recreations of writing rooms are not unusual in and of themselves, academic Nicola Watson points out that a unique approach was taken to preserve *every* aspect of his famous writing shed: 'having carefully killed all the vermin that were thriving in the rotting paper, wood, and upholstery, the conservators hoovered up the dust of thirty years, sterilized it, and then sprinkled it across the reconstructed and relocated whole'.[33] Though the shed has been remade in a new place, it seems the conservators and curators envisioned this re-placing of the original dust as a way of giving authenticity back to the newly contextualised space. While I don't think anyone involved was thinking of this overtly, I can't help but read this as a way of putting Dahl's body back into the room, even if only through years of discarded skin cells. For the critic and academic Steven Connor, dust is intimately related to magic and magical thinking, but also with the idea of 'a body that is as diffuse or scattered as it is possible to be while yet maintaining a minimal or even imaginary cohesion'.[34] Here it seems that dust is a way of imagining that 'diffuse' body, momentarily reconstructed, adding back into the space something that truly 'belonged' to Dahl.

The artist Cornelia Parker was also inspired by dust: her piece *Exhaled Blanket* (1996) projects a sample of the dust and residue from Freud's famous therapeutic couch, thereby exposing its contents to more detailed scrutiny. Of course, the few scant wisps do not really tell us or show us anything more about the couch than we might discover standing in its presence, but the piece hints at our interest in being able to get somehow 'closer' to the objects of our most beloved writer for a more in-depth examination. On the wall, the projected image reveals only the impression of something ubiquitous and banal, mirroring in a way the work of psychoanalysis itself, which enlarges the thoughts, wishes and dreams of the patient, drawing them out of the shadows. But, as with Dahl's dusty residue, can we even see this as truly belonging to Freud? Who can say if what we see on screen actually did belong to him, his couch, or his patients, all these years later?

These objects – Keats's mask, Dahl's and Freud's dust, Woolf's behind glass desk – all give us an insight into the limitations of looking for 'authentic' versions of those authors we admire. Perhaps we shall always chase writers, looking for new ways to get closer to them and their creative impulse. But the preserved writer's room is a site that goes beyond any individual relationship; there remains a tussle between the potential there for a more personal connection with the writers we love, and the knowledge that there is a multitude of others whose endeavours make that possible.

In one afternoon, I visit Mark Twain's home in Connecticut, Lucille Clifton's home in Baltimore, Jane Austen's home in Hampshire, and Victor Hugo's home in Guernsey; I watch a video of a walk-through of Derek Walcott's childhood home in St Lucia. I am moving from country to country, place to place, without leaving my own desk. I had soon realised that I would be able to explore many more places than I had first imagined, even if only virtually, poring over snapshots or tours of desks and bedrooms through the small screen of my laptop, several museums having added these virtual tours or videos during the pandemic. In moments when a large proportion of us were confined in our homes for longer than we had ever been before, other people's houses became more interesting, maybe even increasingly important. Not only as vehicles for our escape, but because perhaps we too were thinking about how we could imbue our homes with meaning: could we, as Woolf suggests, strongly imprint ourselves on our possessions as writers seem to do?

The differences between those spaces I look at seem quite remarkable: Hugo's ornate house overlooking the sea diverging wildly from the Austen cottage, nestled in the green countryside; Lucille Clifton's home felt like the space for comfortable family life, in contrast to the vast sprawl of Mark Twain's many rooms. There was no pattern I could glean, no uniform version of creativity on show: instead, I thought about the lives that had been lived in these spaces. Each visit brought me back to the act of preservation: I wondered if these websites would ensure an even longer life for these houses, providing a kind of parallel version and thereby countering the inevitable process of decay. The tours I navigated with my mouse demonstrate a very different kind of labour, a maintenance of sites and codes, rather than gardens and buildings. As a visitor, I could not touch or get close to Twain's chair or Hugo's chandelier in the rooms I moved through, or easily peer at a portrait or an old photograph that adorned a wall, but only zoom in on increasingly pixelated portions of my screen, and hope to catch glimpses of little details that helped attach that person to that place. Rather than tracing a physical journey that would lead me to these writers, finding directions and checking maps and opening times, I had the strange experience of entering into rooms unknown, and then being able to dismiss them, all with the click of a button. Trite as it may seem, I did not feel I accompanied any of these writers in their spaces; instead I hoovered up information, trying to find their desk in a slightly grainy or blurred image, or some other sign of their life that made these writers, often long dead and feeling far removed from me, more tangible, more real.

In thinking about the limitations of these virtual visits then, perhaps I come to some kind of truth — as Woolf did on her visit to the Brontës — about what these preserved spaces mean to me. They are a way of looking for company, community even. The solitary labour of writing is writ large in these rooms, but in going to visit, with a kind of puppyish and naive enthusiasm, I find the possibilities of companionship, knowing just how many different versions of these spaces have existed, so many writers all working and trying to get their ideas down, their points across, a shared endeavour across years, sometimes centuries. But solitude is, as we have seen in this chapter, always *produced*: these spaces speak with many voices, of curators, of volunteers, as well as our writers and their families. They show us a version of creative solitude that is both ideal and idealised – and that is, potentially, something only of our imagination.

*Joan Didion being filmed and interviewed
in her New York apartment, September 2007.*

Chapter 2

THE WRITER'S ROOM IN PUBLIC

In November 2022, 224 objects belonging to the author and journalist Joan Didion, who had died the previous December, went up for auction. Hosted at the Stair Galleries in New York, Didion's possessions, ranging from heavy furniture to little collections of seashells, were arranged to look lived in, connected, at home with one another. In the words of the critic Sophie Haigney, this auction display was 'set up like an artificial apartment where Joan might have been caught in medias res for a glossy magazine spread'.[1] Various desks, punctuated with typewriters and paperweights, were organised as little imagined scenes of creative possibility nestled in among scenes of domesticity. Where writer's rooms in their original houses, or even preserved in museums, reveal our desire to dwell on the possibility of our authors living, breathing and working, in this estate sale we come to a kind of logical conclusion, where the whole of our writer's life becomes available for public consumption – for purchase – piece by piece.

In Didion's case, part of what many of her fans seemed to admire (and therefore desired to take home with them) was her aesthetic. Over the course of her career, Didion was always associated with glamour, with a kind of writerly aloofness that seems to imply that the world can be worn lightly, like a shawl to be swept off when the weather changes. Whether in long printed skirts, white T-shirts or baggy jumpers, Didion radiated a California cool. This reputation was borne out in the reaction to the auction, and in the days around it, as writers and fans marvelled on Twitter and in articles across the internet about how much people were willing to pay in order to have a little piece of Joan. Tables, books and art all fetched prices into the thousands of dollars, but the sales that baffled many were the three lots of plain, unopened and some plastic-wrapped Moleskines in sensible colours – brown, dark red, black. Yet as Haigney suggests, 'Perhaps that's the whole appeal – to write in a blank space that Didion might once have intended to use herself.'[2] Those notebooks, though close to containing Didion's prose, are overwritten with something else – her ownership – an ownership so strong that any potential words written into them could feel suffused with hers. I thought about the person who bought them, wondering if anything would ever make their way onto the pages, or if they would sit somewhere, an item only to be admired, or shown off at a dinner party. As I scrolled through the catalogue, I wondered what object I would have liked for myself. I dismissed a writing object (too obvious), and instead settled on her trademark Celine sunglasses, completely over-the-top in their largeness, the shape of the lenses wide and round. I imagined they'd allow me a new way of seeing – hers; our lives momentarily intersecting. I, too, couldn't help but fall into that trap of proximity. There was something very alluring about even the more generic objects too: an apron printed with the phrase 'Maybe broccoli doesn't like you either' or a Le Creuset dish. These things that told a story not about her life in writing, but her life as a person.

Academic Rebecca Roach suggests that the 'supposedly private author's study has in fact become one of the most commoditized sites of the writing life in the twentieth century'.[3] This commodification of the writer's room as private property is writ large in Didion's estate sale, but it is one of countless ways that the space has become inextricable from the way we conceive the writer's life. Regardless of the context in which a writer finds themselves talking about their work – lectures, talks, interviews

– questions about the places in which they create that work are almost inescapable. The *Guardian*, picking up on this interest, dedicated an entire series to the topic, entitled simply 'Writers' rooms'. Between 2007 and 2009, a range of authors, including Michael Rosen, Kate Mosse and Seamus Heaney, talked about their writing spaces, offering a history of how they came to be in that place, describing particularly valuable or sentimental objects, offering an account of the pleasures and pains of finding themselves tethered to one room or desk. Across the pond, the *New York Times* ran an almost identical column more sporadically, this time with the chosen writers appearing in an accompanying photograph. At almost every book event I've been to, someone invariably asks about writing locations and I've found myself slightly despairing at these questions asked with such frequency, with seemingly no forum safe. Even during the British writer Hilary Mantel's Reith Lectures on BBC Radio in 2017, the chair Sue Lawley couldn't help but take the opportunity to ask her where she writes.[4] As I listened, I wondered at Lawley's impetus, about what answer Mantel could give that would satisfy her curiosity. There is something very similar in the answers of most writers: their spaces described, ideas about routine, regular writing habits, achievable goals spooling out from there and, more often than not, a nod to the necessity of reading. In Mantel's case, her answer was brief – she could write almost anywhere, but the work was finalised in her house in Budleigh Salterton. A not particularly interesting moment in an otherwise fascinating talk. And yet, these questions about 'where' never seem to get at the crux of what people are really asking: what is writing? Can you tell me the honest truth, they seem to demand, about what it actually is?

In the preserved writer's room, there is always a tension between the status of this as the most secluded and sequestered space in the home, and its more recent visibility and presence in public life. These places of quiet work, where writers are supposed to be diligently focused, have become exposed to society's gaze in their absence. Sometimes, this is dramatised even further, as we saw in Keats House, where the expectation, even the need, to see a writer's space is so strong that the curators have embellished the truth with a writing scene Keats never had and implements he never used. In looking for some explanation of this most mysterious of activities, it seems to me that we start to look for 'proof' of writing in all aspects of the lives of those who do it, understanding everything they do as illustrative of their special status. The French literary critic Roland Barthes famously satirised this idea of the unshakeable identity of the writer who even on holiday can never stop 'being' one. The four walls of the writer's room are not as solid as they might seem; the writer's room bleeds out into the world, as

DeLillo said, so the person carries with them some version of its significance in whatever context they find themselves in.

⌒

The photograph that graces the 12 April 1937 cover of *Time* magazine has Virginia Woolf once more looking out of the frame, but the young girl in the portrait taken by George Charles Beresford in 1902 is gone, and instead a confident woman takes her place, her hair glossy and smoothly parted, her hand held aloft, as if she is about to make a comment in conversation. Alongside the photograph is an article that celebrates Woolf as 'foremost woman author of her day':[5] at fifty-five and having just published her seventh novel, Woolf is an established literary figure at home and internationally. After the writer has given a potted account of Woolf and her work, the article closes on the image of a '[t]all, gaunt, haunted-looking Virginia Woolf' who lives hidden away at Monk's House, 'the picture of a sensitive, cloistered literary woman'.[6] This invocation of Woolf's life is, of course, complicated by the reality of her biography, her many visitors to Monk's House, the joy she took in socialising, in simple drives in her car, but crucially Woolf's entire being is made synonymous here with the sheltered life of the creative, as her multi-dimensional life is replaced with one only of the mind. Huddled in her writer's room, this version of Woolf is intent on making 'a world of her own'.[7] But, as we know, the little room in the garden was not the only place she worked: the article embellishes, simplifies, reaffirming once more the image of the suffering writer ('tall, gaunt, haunted'), her sensitivity making it too much for her to fully inhabit the world that 'we', the readers of the magazine, have no choice but to live in. In this version of the writer's room in public, the author must always retreat if they are to do creative work that matters, remaining in painful solitude.

As we saw in the previous chapter, writer's houses have always been a source of fascination as well as a popular tourist destination; people were heading to the site of the Italian poet Petrarch's house in the fourteenth century and looking for evidence of the life of Shakespeare in Stratford-upon-Avon not long after he died in 1616. This interest in writers' origins was echoed and extended when, around the mid-nineteenth century, it became possible to read the writer in interview, and celebrity culture as we would recognise it today began in earnest, the first celebrity writers in the Western world commonly thought to be Romantic poets such as Lord Byron. The *Strand* magazine, an English monthly publication that started in 1891, had a series of 'Illustrated Interviews' with the great and the good of society, including authors such as Jules Verne and Arthur Conan Doyle, always including an image of the writer's study and desk. The *Idler*, another English magazine edited for much of its time by writer Jerome K. Jerome, had its 'Lions in their Den' column – discussions with writers in situ that feel astonishingly familiar. An 1893 interview with the French writer Emile Zola, conducted by V. R. Mooney, opens by describing Zola's lavishly decorated Parisian home. Mooney then asks Zola about his life, and Zola happily obliges, with talk then moving to writing methods, all accompanied by illustrations of his rooms and portraits of the writer at different ages. The column closes with a line-drawing of Zola, sitting in an ornate high-backed chair, looking pensively at the sheets of paper on his desk, head resting on hand, pen balanced carefully, waiting on his next word; the figure of the writer in deep thought. Like Woolf, the interview presents the solitary writer as a basic, undeniable fact of the writing life. Except for the room that contains Zola himself, the rest of his house – in this vision, at least – is empty.

Interviews from this period helped solidify the mythological status of the writer. In moments of idle thought, I've found I can all too well imagine myself in interview, establishing a witty rapport with someone smart, sharing little titbits from my writing routine, describing my writing room, and perhaps rounding off our conversation with some profound insights into the life of the writer. What I'm really doing is imagining myself speaking in the shared language of the writerly interview, which becomes the shared language for the writer in public, in which the details we read may have the potential for insight or shed light on some reality of writing, but are perhaps really more repeatable than we'd readily admit. The writer is unique, the interview seems to suggest, but that uniqueness is something that could be learned and acquired. After all, as American writer Roxane Gay wonders, maybe our interest in talks and interviews with writers are really about feeling a kinship with them, that 'we want to know that famous writers, they're just like us'.[8]

Being 'just like us' means using the same things that most people use, and in a world of ubiquitous social media, writers are expected to be visible and accessible, both by their publishers and their audiences. In fact, social media allows writers the possibility to behave as everyone does in these online spaces, posting their opinions on politics, on articles, even on other people's books. I've enjoyed the accounts of writers Hari Kunzru and Brandon Taylor on Twitter, their esoteric posting style and their humour; and watched with more trepidation the comments of Joyce Carol Oates, who gained further notoriety when she derided contemporary auto-fiction as mere 'wan little husks',[9] a reference to a proliferation of fragmented, sometimes aphoristic writing across the last decade or so. This digital version of the writer is an addendum to the one we read, arguably not a necessary part of our engagement with the texts they produce. Academic Simone Murray calls the various spaces of online magazines, social media and interview 'the digital literary sphere', a kind of extended and capacious writer's room. For critics including Christian Lorentzen, these other versions of our writers can prove a distraction, suggesting that as a culture we must remember that 'writers are not famous like actors, and shouldn't be under the burden of being as interesting as their books, and the authors of the most interesting books never will be'.[10] For him, there is a pressure for the writer to view *themselves* as a kind of public property, where they have to slough off their real lives in order to become a blander, more marketable product, providing an accompanying narrative to the writing in the form of their public self. Of course, lots of writers, as Oates demonstrates, appear to ignore this demand but there's a tricky balancing act to be performed here: writers must take part in some forms of promotion if they want people to be interested in their work and ultimately buy their books, but what are the limitations? In our imagination, the writer can be both that person sequestered away at the desk and *also* fully out in the world, giving talks, posting on Instagram and making videos for TikTok. Perhaps writers feel duty-bound to reveal themselves more and more, not only giving glimpses into their writing rooms, but their whole houses, their whole lives.

This feeling of intimacy can also emerge when writers move beyond being 'mere' producers of books, into other realms. Some writers are elevated to a kind of public intellectual, called upon to comment on events of the world, even on subjects on which they may not be particularly well-versed. No other writer seems to fit the bill more clearly than Zadie Smith. Much has been written about her extraordinary rise to fame, of the selling of her debut novel, *White Teeth*, in her early twenties, just before the new millennium, for an advance of £250,000. Her unique style, comic and breezy at points but also sensitive to the intimate structures of family and identity, and the sheer ambitious reach of that first novel, meant that for many Smith seemed to have precious insight into *how things were*. Her youth and precociousness also added to this; how could someone so young have so much to say?

Emerging from this acclaim is a particular writerly identity that, for better or worse, Smith now holds. But even in the very earliest days of her writing Smith seemed to struggle with this role: in an interview on Charlie Rose's chat show in 2000 to promote the publication of *White Teeth* in America, her response to his opening question about her new-found fame was immediately to mention the safety of her writer's room: 'I spent two years in my room and got used to that kind of life. The way publishing is these days, there's a different side to your job which involves going out into the world and doing this sort of thing.'[11] Twelve years later, in an interview with fellow writer Christopher Bollen, her position hasn't altered: 'The bit that involves the public life I could not really tolerate and cannot really tolerate. I just can't get used to the idea of being somebody unreal in people's minds. I can't live my life like that. And it's just anathema to being a writer.'[12] Smith, as Lorentzen describes other writers, seems to feel that push and pull of celebrity keenly, wanting to avoid developing that seemingly personal relationship with the people who read her, becoming 'somebody unreal' as she puts it. Smith seems to deal with her dislike of this feeling by underplaying any kind of privileged position for the writer. The novelist and critic Lauren Oyler notes that part of Smith's writerly identity is presenting herself as 'a kind of relatable everywoman, or at least "no authority". She is constantly making fun of herself, or putting herself down, or expressing wonder at the achievements of other artists and writers.'[13] But of course, '[t]hat she is not entirely this everywoman but also an international literary celebrity . . . is a dualism she resists more than the others she wears proudly'.[14] And though Smith may feel hesitant and uncomfortable about being in 'public life', she has increasingly participated in it through the subjects of her writing. Her essay collection from 2018, *Feel Free*, contains her thoughts on Brexit, Jeremy Corbyn and Facebook; 2020's *Intimations* was written at the beginning of the Covid-19 pandemic and gave space to a similarly broad range of topics. In these essays she unavoidably takes a stand, critiques politicians or governments, and reflects on societal ills, often positioning herself as a voice of the sensible middle, not looking to rock the boat: as the writer and critic Andrea Long Chu describes, Smith has an 'almost involuntary tendency to reframe all political questions as "human" ones'.[15] She is, for better or worse, placing herself in the public sphere as someone to be called upon to do exactly what she has repeatedly expressed discomfort over. Here once more is the paradox of the contemporary writer, a person with whom many of us feel a strange kind of intimacy, even at the expense of the desires of the writer themselves. Zola's empty rooms have become populated by the world.

Even more overtly resistant to celebrity culture is literary phenomenon Sally Rooney. The Irish writer of four novels, most recently 2024's *Intermezzo*, is considered something of a 'representational' writer, in the same way that Smith was in the early 2000s, capturing not the mood of post-2000s Britain but the anxieties of the generation who grew up during it. Rooney's writing has been astonishingly popular: *Intermezzo* sold over 40,000 copies in its first week of release. She occupies a unique position in contemporary writing – known globally, her work translated into forty languages – and yet is at pains to emphasise how much she views the business of writing, the work at the desk and the publishing industry as quite separate. There are no accompanying pictures of her, pen in hand, for 'At Home With' style features or promotion because she does not invite that type of scrutiny, describing herself as 'paranoid about [her] personal life'.[16] In fact, the interviews that Rooney does agree to are accompanied with photographs of the author outside, sitting on a picnic table or on a sandy dune, seemingly far away from her desk. In a more recent interview, Rooney explains her dismay as functioning as a 'type' in contemporary writing: 'I often feel discouraged by the publishing industry. I often see novels marketed as 'for fans of Sally Rooney'. I find that so dispiriting – the invention of a certain type of person for the purposes of book marketing. And it makes me feel complicit in the commodification and cheapening of literary culture.'[17] I should note here that, of course, there is a difference between the writer and the machinery around them. Rooney's work, as we've seen with other writers, belongs to the reading public that surrounds it as much as the writer herself. Where some in publishing could say that invoking her name on the cover of a book by another writer functions as a shorthand, a way of helping readers find other writing they might like, others (including Rooney herself) see the way that constant comparison between writers serves to narrow, not widen, reading tastes: if every book becomes a 'possible Sally Rooney book', then every writer could be Sally Rooney. By denying the intrusion into her life, her home and her writing space, Rooney resists her own marketisation. Clearly echoing the comments of Christian Lorentzen, she avoids using her public platform as a means of presenting herself as an extension of her books; instead she focuses on drawing attention to issues she cares about, such as abortion rights in Ireland or, more recently, the plight of the people of Gaza.

In the figure of Rooney, we see a writer drawing a distinct line about where the life and work of the writer must take place. Of course, some writers shun the spotlight altogether. Much has been made of the so-called 'disappearance' of J. D. Salinger from public life, after the immense success of his work *Catcher in the Rye* in the 1950s. Thomas Pynchon, best known as the author of the postmodernist tome *Gravity's Rainbow*, is, in some ways, *more* famous because of the very fact so few photographs exist of him; he has, however, appeared on three episodes of *The Simpsons*, voicing himself twice in the episodes 'Diatribe of a Mad Housewife' and 'All's Fair in Oven War', and hovering in the background of 'Moe'N'a Lisa'. Each time, the show writers make fun of his elusiveness as he wears a paper-bag decorated with a question mark over his head. In recent years, this desire to 'unmask' an unseen writer took a more sinister turn, when journalist Claudio Gatti pored through financial records in order to find out the identity of Italian writer Elena Ferrante. Gatti named who he thought Ferrante was, triumphantly declaring the outcome of his investigations (something I won't do here), but his actions were met with horror, as an enormous invasion of privacy motivated by misogyny. I love Pynchon's playfulness, and Ferrante's refusal to reveal herself. These writers ask for a different relationship between the reader and writer, one based on their words and not their cultural identity or their performance of their 'writerliness'. Both writers refuse us the image of themselves hard at work, whether tethered to a desk or working completely haphazardly. I see great freedom in this, where writers challenge the need to give insight into their process, and only their books evidence all that labour.

We can blame part of our continuing fascination with the writer's room on its seemingly endless depictions in film and in television. My mother is an enthusiast of old Hollywood, and so I had an early education in versions of life that were more exciting, more romantic, more saturated in Technicolor. As a family we watched a lot of Hitchcock, *Vertigo* and *Rear Window*, and films with Cary Grant, *Charade* and *Father Goose*. My sister and I would put on double-bills of Rock Hudson and Doris Day films, with slightly risqué titles such as *Lover Come Back* and *Pillow Talk*, and settle down for the afternoon. Later, I started to drift into what I felt were the more serious realms of the self-reflexive. I became interested in a certain kind of backstage story, movies about actors or writers, where the mechanisms of Hollywood were on display: my favourite was *All About Eve*, which was ostensibly about the careers of theatre actors, but was clearly mappable onto film too. Bette Davis's wild and prickly Margo Channing, worrying about ageing and her career, finds herself at the mercy of the conniving Eve Harrington, who goes after her roles, and eventually her husband. I was enraptured by the flashing eyes of Davis, and by the great crescendos of her emotion, but I loved even more the way *All About Eve* showed that art is made by talented, fallible, arrogant people and through so much unacknowledged work, choreographed and managed by teams of other people, producers, directors and writers, who shape what we eventually see.

Still, I could never have guessed just how self-obsessed Hollywood really was, and how many film scripts had their stars play not actors but writers, trying and failing in front of typewriters – no doubt in echo of their creators. The studio system of the major production companies was hungry for material, as increasing numbers flocked to film at the beginning of the twentieth century. Yet the rapid expanse left many writers and directors jaded by the process, reflected in those movie-writer figures in the films of the 1940s and 1950s, lamenting the low-quality work they were paid handsomely to produce. Humphrey Bogart's Dixon Steele, the protagonist of Nicholas Ray's *In a Lonely Place*, does not want to adapt into a screenplay the bad novel he's been given by his agent, and cannot find any motivation to complete the job; roaming around Hollywood, drinking at his club, he seems to resent screenwriting altogether, telling an actress acquaintance that he makes a point of never seeing the movies he pens. When he is implicated in the murder of a young woman, his new neighbour Laurel Gray (played by Gloria Grahame) becomes his alibi, and through their meeting his love of writing is revitalised. In one scene, after Laurel and Dixon are married, the couple are visited by Mel Lippman, Dixon's agent, who is thrilled to see his formerly morose client creating new scripts with such fervency. Where earlier Dixon and his desk were bathed in darkness, the chiaroscuro of film noir exaggerating the despair he feels, in these later scenes Laurel and Mel watch him from a distance in a room bathed in sunlight, as if rays of inspiration now shine on him as he huddles over his paper, completely engrossed in his task. Laurel relays to Mel that having already been tied to his desk for days, her husband hasn't stopped working all night. Through the enlivening effects of love, Dixon Steele becomes the ideal writer – a ceaseless word machine.

Many films depict this contrast, between awful, painful writer's block, and the sudden outpouring of creative energy, as a central tenet of the plot. *Adaptation* (2002), written by Charlie Kaufman and directed by Spike Jonze, dramatises this idea of the unproductive author by including two contrasting examples, one with the name Charlie Kaufman, who can't do the work, and one, his invented identical twin Donald, who can, both played by Nicholas Cage. Though Charlie has had successes (his opening lunch with a film executive, played by Tilda Swinton, makes clear that this Charlie, like the real Kaufman, wrote *Being John Malkovich*) his writing set up is far from glamorous: as he sits hunched over a low table, his body looking enormous and uncomfortably wedged into a too-small chair, he distracts himself from beginning with thoughts of muffins and coffee. Like Dixon Steele, Charlie is trying to adapt a work for film, not a novel but a piece of non-fiction: *The Orchid Thief* by Susan Orlean. This is a long and complex essay in the first person, with many deviations, and he cannot find the angle from which to write the screenplay. His brother Donald, who is staying in his apartment, decides seemingly on a whim that he too will become a screenwriter, but he doesn't follow the model of his brother, instead choosing often to lie on the floor, eating sandwiches and reading books about story structure while smiling placidly. When he is at the typewriter, he is accompanied by a pretty girl he is seeing, who willingly discusses the beats of the screenplay and compliments him on his cleverness.

Donald finds writing miraculously easy because he follows the rules of genre, introducing twists that Charlie finds derivative. In Donald, Kaufman conjures not only a chipper and industrious version of himself (Donald seems always to be working, though it is mostly off-screen) but also a more sexually confident, more *alive* version. Kaufman both explores and satirises the suffering writer, exploring self-effacingly whether some of this suffering is self-inflicted.

The notion of the uninspired author is not limited in its targets on film: one of the most amusing comes in the opening credits of *Shakespeare in Love*: a handsome, well-shaved man, played by Joseph Fiennes, sits at his desk, his shirt opened alluringly to midchest. Our writer balls up a piece of parchment that lands next to a skull – a nod, no doubt, to the famous skull of Yorrick in *Hamlet* – looking thoroughly unimpressed with himself. As the film title moves across the screen, so too does the quill of the writer, revealing that he is none other than William Shakespeare – but this Shakespeare, we realise, is not in a fit of creative flow but is instead writing out his signature in varying spellings and then crossing them through, as if negating each of these possible versions of himself. Though Shakespeare looks serious, we are invited to laugh at the sheer absurdity of the idea of the most famous of writers experiencing anything even resembling writer's block.

He too is eventually spurred on to new creative avenues by the possibility of love in the form of Gwyneth Paltrow's stage actor. But, as with Dixon Steele, the addition of another person provides the inspiration; the writer remains the solitary genius.

Re-imagining the writing process of Shakespeare is partly possible because we don't really know how he wrote or have an authoritative version of his writing space to use as a touchstone. It is a work of imagination. To be a writer in the twenty-first century, as we've seen, is to be accompanied by a great many other parallel forms of visibility beyond the book itself, and in fact, we could argue a hyper-visibility, not just of where and how you work, but of how you live. Michaela Coel's 2020 television series *I May Destroy You* is not only about the writing process, but also the visibility of life online, and the greater pressures in being a creator of colour. The central character, Arabella (played by Coel), has signed a book deal with the publisher Henry House after the popularity of her first book, *Chronicles of a Fed-up Millennial*, which she released for free online. Her publisher wants to harness the audience she has cultivated, demanding she speak 'authentically' – specifically as a young Black woman. Arabella struggles to write, but when she is drugged and raped, the programme swerves from the demands of creative life to question if it is possible to narrate, and hopefully overcome, a horrendous trauma.

Across the series, we return frequently to Arabella's bedroom, the setting for her private as well as writing life. Here, among her clothes and possessions, Arabella finally finds the possibility of ending her story, communicated to us — the voyeuristic viewer — through her ordering and reordering of Post-it notes on her wall, in not one but three distinct versions, shown one after another. Coel asserts the impossibility of tying up the strands of the narrative, instead sitting with its ambiguity; to have produced one simple ending, she seems to suggest, would be to delineate artificially something infinitely complex — which is, of course, what we ask of our writers every day. The ending also shows a writer in the flushes of unceasing creativity, in a writing room that is embedded within the scene of her life. Though the show critiques what others expect of Black voices, satirising the publishing industry and its accompanying commodification of 'authenticity', Coel's version of writing labour is quite distinctly based in the challenges of being a writer of varying intersecting identities that are a source of pride and meaning but that can also be weaponised against them. Yet even amid these gnarly realities, the show seems to suggest that there is a way of finding beautiful, transformative creativity.

I wonder why writing is so often presented as being characterised by horrible stops that feel painful, almost dangerous. The ideal that film and television often shows us is of a writing life that is continuous: when writing is happening 'properly', these scenes tell us, it is uncontainable, rushing out in a force. The spaces of writing then are to facilitate the smooth transformation of ideas that are 'inside' to become 'outside', placed finally and definitively on the page. These moments of pause are not shown to be part and parcel of writing, but instead something to be feared: all of these versions of the writer on screen show any hesitancy in creation as something intrinsically negative.

What would it look like, I wonder, if everyone who had ever aimed to write allowed a camera into their work space? I think of my own writing, sometimes embarrassingly full of stops and starts. Hilary Mantel noted in an interview with the *Guardian* that she was often met with pity by people who thought the large gaps between her novels showed her to suffer from writer's block whereas, in reality, she had been working solidly, countering, 'I've been like a factory.'[18] Rather than assuming that her supposed 'silences' came from the extensive research needed to produce her novels about Thomas Cromwell, readers thought a gap in a publishing schedule reflected that she was *not* working.

Writing, like all work, cannot continue unceasingly. The writer Geoff Dyer notes that 'I think it's just a lazy-thinking kind of cliché, this idea of writer's block.' Maybe when writing doesn't happen it simply means, as Dyer says, 'I just haven't had anything to say.'[19] This seems to me to be a much more useful way of envisioning these blocks: sometimes words don't come because they simply aren't there. There is no 'block' at all. In my own practice, moments of pause are not only frequent but crucial; the most predictable surprise of writing is the way that ideas will suddenly knit together in a completely different context, while I'm walking, or reading something on another topic, or cleaning the bathroom, or, indeed, watching a film. I'd be terrified to experience the overwhelming torrent of words and thoughts that characterises the idealised version of writing, as it seems to suggest that if I don't catch them quickly enough those ideas may well disappear.

Of course, there is another dimension to this, where even having writer's block, or the idea of being 'blocked', feeds into a particular version of a (writing) life. As the Mexican writer Brenda Navarro noted, 'Writer's block is a thing for men with time.'[20] That romance of creative block speaks to its inverse, that words can and should come streaming out unceasingly, and that there would be no barrier to a person recording them. For many writers, time and space do not work in this way: when writing time is carved from other places in the day, the notion of a 'block' is simply not possible. The work, regardless of the writer's situation, their energy, their sleep levels, when it needs to be finished, gets done.

THE WRITER'S ROOM IN PUBLIC

What does the writer look like and how can we *know* who is and is not a writer? In an image-saturated culture, there are many more opportunities for us to communicate that we are, or would like to be, writers. In April 2023, *Granta* magazine announced their list of twenty writers under forty said to represent the 'Best of British Novelists'. *Granta* puts together this list every ten years, and it is often populated with writers who go on to become very well known, including Zadie Smith, Julian Barnes and Salman Rushdie. A special issue of the magazine is always published alongside the announcement, which includes writing by the twenty selected, as well as portraits of each of them, taken in this latest iteration by photographer Alice Zoo. Zoo's portraits are by no means uniform, and she has captured these writers in different poses and places, some sitting comfortably on sofas, some outside against a wall or nestled among foliage, while others are shot in close up, glancing out of the frame, with a slight smile or a serious look of intention. Unsurprisingly, my eye was struck by the photograph Zoo had taken of Tom Crewe, writer of the novel *The New Life* (2023): smartly dressed in dark trousers and jacket, with a little bright swipe of red sock, he sits upright in a black office chair next to a cluttered metal desk. On it rest many books, some organised into piles, one of which looks a little precarious, balanced right at the desk's edge. Peeking just out of the left of the frame is an edition of Samuel Beckett's play *Footfalls*, replete with a photograph of the playwright in serious profile, his elegant head atop a smart grey suit; on the floor are the several volumes that make up the Taschen catalogue of the complete work of Impressionist painter Claude Monet. More books are strewn about, almost totally obscuring the inviting green chaise longue that projects towards the viewer, the covers out of focus or at an angle so that we cannot read them. There are prints on the walls, a sculpture behind Crewe himself, and more frames underneath the desk, turned away from us and resting against the walls. The photograph is lit by the white light coming in from the sash window that sits behind the writer's head; light, the image seems to suggest, illuminates this scene of hard graft. The image is remarkably communicative, telling us much about Crewe himself: he is serious, he is studious, but he isn't fussy. The room feels contingent, changeable: the books on the desk and the chaise longue that are there today may well not be tomorrow, as his subject or his interests change. The room is in the flush of creativity, and creativity is always unplanned and altering.

I wondered why Crewe had selected this backdrop as the one to represent him; or actually, I wondered why *more* of the writers hadn't chosen to represent themselves nestled in their rooms. Some had chosen to show themselves in repose and at ease – I was quite charmed by Eleanor Catton's cosy-looking socks in her portrait and Eliza Clark's choice to sit on the floor, her phone prominent in the foreground – but Crewe foregrounds his room as a crucial part of his writerly identity. Knowing that the *Granta* list would have much publicity and fanfare, I wondered how much the other writers had worried about curating their appearance.

I've studied so many author portraits, looking to see if I can find a common denominator that suggests them as writers, often it is the setting itself – the chair, or the desk, or the props that decorate the image, the inclusion of a notebook, or a typewriter. There are some that for me feel iconic: the images of Susan Sontag, with her characteristic white stripe in her hair, a cigarette held loftily above her typewriter; the French writer Georges Perec with his voluminous curls, always looking mischievous and energetic, and sometimes accompanied by a black cat draped around his neck; Zadie Smith with her exacting hair wraps and immaculate lipstick. These images seem to exude *something* I can't quite put my finger on, some unapologetic sense of the idiosyncrasy of the person themself.

On a cold and misty January day, I half-wondered if I should try to channel any of these while I had my own author portrait taken by the photographer Sophie Davidson. She patiently tried to distract me as we wandered around Walthamstow Village looking for a suitable place for me to plant myself and pose. I had worried in advance of the session, thinking about what to wear and how I should orient my body; I've never found it easy to have my photograph taken, always being terribly unsure of how to set my features. I had thought about being photographed at my desk, but it would have felt a little too obvious, given the subject of this book. Sophie tried to cajole me into looking slightly more cheerful, and to smile with a bit more lightness, but my face stayed resolutely grim. I was grateful to be so wrapped up in my slightly weather-beaten burgundy coat, and tomato-red scarf, as if they were a kind of protection from the embarrassment I felt. My uncertainty was showing; away from my desk or my books, what proof did I have that I was a writer, that my work was worth reading, except for the fact I had paid for a photographer to have my picture taken? It all felt very circular, as if I was jumping the gun; shouldn't the book come before the author photograph?

I found, though, that the process was an important one, that getting the portrait taken signalled I was beginning to think about what my life might look like in writing, that I could move beyond worrying about what objects I kept around me and how authentic my room looked, into trickier realms of self-confidence, self-belief. I had the idea that I would be both myself and also 'the writer', as if

THE WRITER'S ROOM IN PUBLIC

those two things were at a distance from one another. I had envisioned an image that could show me transformed into some kind of glamorous artist. But, of course, I would always end up with an image of myself, undoubtedly still me, but another version in which I asserted that I had things to say and ideas worth communicating. And although I felt as if I had been self-regarding in presuming to get my author picture taken, I was also being practical; after all, the author portrait is part of the writer's arsenal, accompanying book announcements and articles, printed on book jackets – if you flick to the back of this book, you'll see just what I mean. Even in the earliest days of printing, drawings of writers would often accompany manuscripts, as a way of conceiving of the 'author', the image of the person functioning as a signature. We see this even in the case of Shakespeare: the 'First Folio', the initial authoritative collection of the playwright's work published posthumously in 1623, is printed with an engraving by Martin Droeshout, and though other portraits and busts exist of Shakespeare, it is probably the only authenticated image of him. It is remarkably similar to a portrait we might see today, with the author wearing a serious but not surly expression, facing three-quarters towards the viewer. In Brian Dillon's book *I Am Sitting in a Room*, he compares a range of portraits from writers such as Vladimir Nabokov and William F. Buckley and finds that in each there is a kind of self-consciousness and awkwardness in their posing that communicates the difficulty of making one's body read as 'writer'. Dillon looks at a different image of Sontag, another I too have admired, cigarette in hand, book piles a little too neatly arranged, and wonders:

> Is Sontag really, I mean *really*, sitting sunlit and assured beneath a lovely vintage advertisement for Olivetti typewriters? It is all too much and yet: I forgive her. She probably needed this level of awkwardly erudite self-invention, and she does nothing to deny the necessary ruse.[21]

It's comforting to know that even those writers who are undoubtedly categorised as 'writers' in our minds, through what they've published, their cultural position, and their lasting reputation, cannot fully hide the problems that self-presentation poses. We are all inventing ourselves, all the time. Writer Emily Cooper, whose author portrait was taken by photographer and publisher Robin Silas Christian in preparation for the publication of her first poetry collection in 2021, is pleased with the image she ended up with 'because I'm looking directly at the camera, not quite confrontationally, but in a way that I feel captures something of my humour'.[22] For her, a negotiation needs to happen between being a 'writer' (with all the baggage that that may hold) and maintaining her sense of self.

For Emily, just as for myself, a portrait taken at the desk would be too much, too overtly *staged*.

I think there is also an issue with how much we want to perform our creativity, to signal to other people we are interesting, that they are catching us as we take a brief break from our writer's room, before we dive back in that scene of tranquillity and industry. I've often played a game when I am out in London to see if I can spot writers wearing a uniform of middle-class artistry: boxy chore jackets, wide-legged trousers, shirts in practical materials such as cotton and canvas, round glasses. Most of these items, in their simplicity, directly riff on the uniforms of manual labourers and factory workers; in this new context, these uniforms speak to not only the efforts of the body but the efforts of the mind. Academic Justin Russell Greene explores how writers' attire can be communicative not just for what it tells the writer about themselves, but for what it will tell readers. He finds, for example, that '[Jonathan] Franzen's attire in his author photograph for *The Corrections* (2001) brands him as the consummate professional with the clothes he wears: a sport coat and a white-collared shirt'.[23] Franzen had styled himself somewhat as a 'defender' of the literary, famously decrying Oprah Winfrey's book club for its cheapening of print culture after she included *The Corrections* in her selection – he was, he signalled, above the books she normally picked, and he wanted, he explained in one interview, to court a more male audience.[24] The professionalism of his picture, then, communicates not only how 'serious' he is about his writing as work, but also the industry as a whole; I would suggest far too serious, and at the expense of adequate respect of many different kinds of readers.

Of course, not all writers are interested in adopting recognisable clothes that mark them out as 'creative'. As Rosemary Hill asks, 'Why should writers mind about clothes? More than any other profession they spend their most productive hours alone. They can wear anything – or nothing – and nobody is any the wiser.'[25] Yet I'm not sure if that's entirely true, not for me anyway. More often than not, if I'm at home, I'll be wearing something casual and comfortable, some pyjama bottoms and a comfortable cotton shirt, but there'll be times when I find myself wanting to dress up, doing something to my hair or putting on some mascara. There is a relationship between clothing and what you tell the world – of intention and purpose. I've realised over the years that my interest in workwear partly stems from its simplicity, its smartness; I feel somehow that I take myself more seriously in the simple act of putting on a blouse.

Newspapers and magazines sometimes offer articles in which they examine the look of a writer, frequently women such as some of the touchstones of this book, Joan Didion and Virginia Woolf, breaking down every aspect of their appearance, from their shoes to their hair. I've even come across a very amusing WikiHow article with advice on how to look like a writer, which encourages interested readers to 'wear mysterious, artsy things' and 'always smell of something slightly nostalgic'.[26] In these versions of the writer, all it takes is for us to wake up one day with an indistinct desire and we can make ourselves seem creative, proximate somehow to a potential writer's life. But alongside that desire must come a certain ability to read the signifiers of class. In November 2018, an account was started on Twitter that was met with simultaneous glee and horror by so-called 'Lit Twitter': Bougie London Literary Woman. A woman in her late twenties working in an indeterminate creative field, Bougie London Literary Woman was sophisticated, well read and well fed. I read through the tweets with increasing delight: 'Wild about my new culottes, which will be just the thing for flaneusing around Broadway market in search of intrigue and bluebells Sunday week';[27] 'Out for a brisk morning stroll. How am I to resist the fishmonger when its windows are so lavishly silvered with bream?'[28] Some readers worried that the account maligned femininity, that it was written by a spurned man (the creators of the account, writer Imogen West-Knights and her unnamed collaborator, later assured us of the contrary by adding a disclaimer to the bio) and that it was too mean-spirited. I was shocked that anyone could have taken this so personally. Perhaps some were upset about this account because of the far-reaching tentacles of its critique; not only did Bougie London Literary Woman announce what she was reading, but also what smells she liked, or what she was eating, all rendered in her distinctive florid prose. She even tweeted about her visits to the British Library; everything she posted was in conversation with everything else, all a question of taste, and taste, like language, is learned, strengthened and continually acquired. The fact that people felt attacked gives an important insight into the minutiae of middle-class values and aesthetic preferences. These intersecting areas of life coalesced in this account with extraordinary precision because they so closely described real lives. Bougie London Literary Woman, regardless of how funny or irritating we may have found it at the time, was a satire of class, as well as those who'd be described as 'literary'. To take it personally was to totally misunderstand the satire – class is not personal. When the conversation came up at events or over coffee, as it invariably did, I always said that it seemed that everyone needed to read the French sociologist Pierre Bourdieu whose extensive work on class demonstrated its unshakeable connection to taste, preference and the activities we participate in; even those most insignificant aspects of our preferences could be understood this way. I realised it wouldn't take much for me to be identified as Bougie London Literary Woman.

But of course, there is the gap between the look and the reality — those who might be interested in harnessing a bookish, writerly aesthetic might not really have any real desire to do the work that goes along with it. After all, though she represents herself as a writer, Bougie London Literary Woman rarely actually does it (though I would love to read a full-length work by her). When, in 2017, there was much coverage about David Cameron's purchase of a shepherd's hut in which he was to write his forthcoming Brexit memoir, it seemed to me to be a logical conclusion of this desire to *seem* writerly, albeit from a completely unexpected place. Cameron's hut is thought to have cost £25,000, made by a company that specialises in luxury shepherd's huts (seemingly a contradiction in terms) inspired by Victorian design; each hut is insulated with sheep's wool, clad in either metal or featheredge, and painted in colours by the high-end paint company Farrow and Ball. Cameron told reporters that he and his children bickered about its ownership, though it seems that the hut was designed and bought for the express purpose of hosting the ex-PM while he produced what would turn out to be the over-700-page account of his time in office, as well as a precis of the Brexit he brought about but didn't resolve. The shepherd's hut seemed to be designed to present him publicly as an author, while simultaneously sloughing off the more unpalatable aspects of his privilege. By making the writing space – and by extension him – cuddly with sheep's wool and painting it non-threatening, muted shades, perhaps it was a means of asserting an (on the surface) rough-and-ready approach to the writing, not done while ensconced in the dark wood of the study, but proximate with the open air, with a window from which to look from and brood. Cameron was attempting to signal some kind of literary prowess with his shed. Or perhaps, more specifically, he was acknowledging his familiarity with the idea that to be a successful writer one must have a designated space within which to do it. Yet though Virginia Woolf mentioned money, she never discussed the possibility of a faux-vintage shepherd's hut when it came to a room of one's own.

At the same time as lamenting the seemingly endless public questions about the ideal writer's space, I wonder how many writers still long for one. Not only are these images available in our imagination, but we are only ever a quick Google away from the perfect but unattainable room: the atmospheric writing shed of Dylan Thomas, looking over the water in Laugharne in Wales, or the food writer Michael Pollan's beautiful lodge with a long low desk and vaulted ceiling, nestled among the trees in the Connecticut countryside.

And we can easily find out that the Scottish writer Ali Smith writes in 'a small, two-storey brick row house off a back street in Cambridge, England, a few doors along from a similar house, also small, where she lives with her partner'.[29] Versions of the good writing life can feel perilously close.

For many millennial writers, born in the 1980s and 1990s, and entering adulthood with the internet, there is a definitive sense that one particular version of a creative career, one that might lead to second houses or custom-made lodges, has passed us by – a version with large advances and better book coverage in the broadsheets. Today, these writers are commenting more overtly on the conditions that have brought about their work: Raven Leilani, author of *Luster*, wrote her novel while studying on an MFA programme, as well as working in publishing, with a side gig as a food delivery driver for Postmates. The narrator of *Luster*, Edie, also works in publishing, and when she loses that role similarly turns to a delivery job, all the while feeling the desperate urge to paint. Edie's life is forcefully split between trying to make money and trying to find ways to do the things that give her life meaning, and Leilani never shies away from the contradiction pulling taut between the two. Even more, Leilani asserts that it is crucial she give adequate space to that intractable problem within her fiction, commenting in one interview, 'Money is extremely important . . . I personally need to know how characters eat and pay rent.'[30] She is not alone in her commitment to talking publicly about artmaking; in recent years a remarkable number of writers, including Claire-Louise Bennett and Hannah Regel, have published novels in which young protagonists want to write or make art but face impediments of varying kinds. Yet these aren't people who are 'blocked' sitting at desks, suffering because they are jaded by bad material like Dixon Steele or taking their work slightly too seriously like Charlie Kaufman; instead, blockages come simply as the stuff of life, the boring business of getting by. Though Sally Rooney may resist the commodification of the writer in her own life, almost all of her books contain characters who are indeed writers, with no desks or messy piles of paper in sight. Where some slated Rooney for making writing look too easy (Becca Rothfeld writes acerbically, 'If you are a writer in a Rooney novel, you are sure to be discovered without going to any great lengths to promote yourself. You are sure to write beautifully without agonizing over your work'[31]), I wonder if instead, Rooney kept the labour of writing noticeably unseen to stop the possibility of fetishisation in its tracks.

Though I critique the way we try to purchase our writers, I am not immune to participating in it. To add to my spoils from Freud's house, and my picture of Woolf's desk, I add a postcard of the writer's desk from the Keats House, arranged differently from the iteration on display at my visit. On my many trips to the William Morris Gallery, I've purchased baubles and pillows and cards in some of his plentiful beautiful prints. At the Carlyle House there was nothing to buy, so I took pictures; on virtual tours I couldn't buy anything either, so I took screengrabs. In all the writer interviews I've read, I'm judging or lusting after the studies and offices and kitchens described or depicted. The sheer volume of these spaces can't help but encourage this sense of relating oneself always to what's on display. Where I might think I'm trying to borrow some of the writer's lustre – and hoping it will rub off on my work, or filling in those blank pages of Didion's notebooks – in truth I'm doing something a little more sinister, something more akin to theft. I'm bringing the outside world of authenticated, credentialled writers into my own space, where I'm less certain of my status. I'm looking to populate my own writing space with an amalgam of those people who have officially and publicly reached the status of 'writer'.

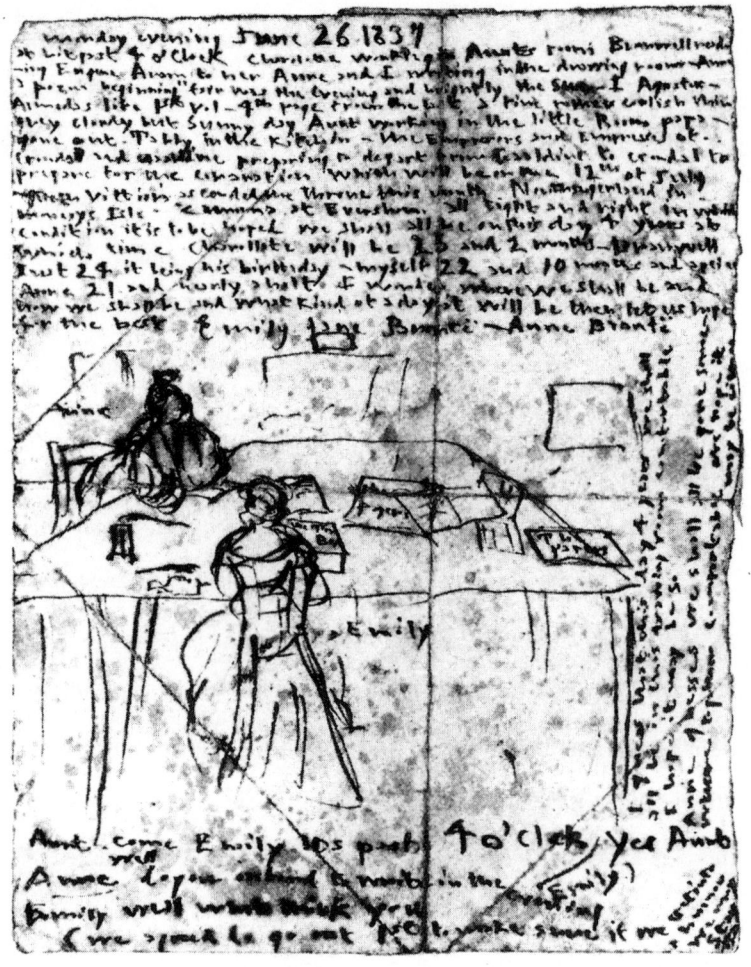

Emily and Anne Brontë at work at the family's dining table, in a sketch from Emily's diary, June 1837.

Chapter 3

SHARED SPACES

I spent many years looking for a place where I could write. In the second year of my PhD, I wandered round London, unsure of where best to work. I had a desk in my tiny bedroom, transplanted from its former life in my parents' house, but the desk didn't do its job; I found that I was still regularly procrastinating, unable to concentrate, to find my flow. Looking back, perhaps the problem was the proximity to my bed, something about the angle of the light from the window. I still can't say. But what I did know then was that I needed somewhere that was outside my own four walls. I began by trying places in east London, heading to Bethnal Green to see if it was still as ramshackle and lively as it had been when I was a teenager looking for vintage clothes.

I found it very much changed, the shops now with polished signage and the uniform interiors speaking the visual language of gentrification. I chose a cake shop, selecting a large slice of red velvet to keep me running on sugar as I tried to focus on understanding the writing of J. M. Coetzee, something I probably never achieved.

It was after someone I met at a conference recommended the British Library that I realised there was a space in which I could work and not have to pay for the privilege. Though I knew about the building, I had discounted it as an option. I was intimidated by the infrastructure, the card that was needed to enter the reading rooms, and nervous about my credentials as a researcher, my ability to do the necessary concentrated work that the building suggested; I worried I wasn't serious enough.

At that point I lived a quick train journey away, and so one day I set off, looking for another kind of writing room, for privacy among other people. I don't remember my first time in the building, nor what I did on those tentative trips, but I do know that I didn't find my rhythm in the place quickly. I could see so many others around me who seemed to have better working habits and sturdier powers of concentration. I often found myself lost in the possibility of the space, in the multiplicity of the books I could order, the many different directions I could mine, but without a sense of where to begin. Gradually, as I got used to the discipline of researching and writing, I began to see myself as a library-goer, bringing snacks, knowing where I could get cheap filter coffee, and finding a desk in a reading room – I preferred the vast space of Humanities 1 over the more intimate Humanities 2, and felt a fraud in Rare Books – at which I could sit for many hours.

I got into a routine with friends also doing PhDs, looking for a companionable 30 minutes (or more likely longer) in which we could shoot the breeze, muck around or worry about what we were doing – together. Other people, I began to realise, were crucial to my experience of the library, to my experience of writing: not just the balm they provided in socialising, but their very presence. The loud announcement of the opening hours of the building and the wheels of the trolleys heaving books around provided one kind of backdrop, but the majority of the sounds I came to associate with the space were made by other people, throat-clearing and coughing, rustling of notebooks, the creaks of shoes on carpet. Though on each trip I left my house alone with my intentions, every time I took a step into the reading room I entered into a unique community of other writers. Ten years later, I still feel the sense of relief that comes with seeing other faces, serious and determined, all around me. Sometimes, there are even monks or priests working alongside me, and I can't help but imagine these men as modern

THE WRITER'S ROOM

St Jeromes. Being in this library, I can find my groove in the way I can't at home. There are no chores to do here and less potential for distraction (though people-watching is, of course, a dangerous pastime). In the library, I can wear a costume of studiousness until it becomes who I am.

The reading rooms here can prompt a lot of strong feeling: some friends of mine cannot stand its quiet, the feeling of being observed, the rules one must follow. I find the various directions are almost second nature to me, but at first I always worried about doing the right thing, as if I would be found out as an interloper in a space for other people so much more suited to study and writing than me. Having now worked within this space for so long, I have come to rely on these rules as a way of understanding how to be in the space, and how to undertake the work of writing. The reading room is based on shared participation in quiet; if anyone deviates from this, the precious mood of the room is shattered. Moments when the equilibrium is disturbed can feel jarring: I was once given the shock of my life when a man had fallen asleep and started producing honking snores; other times, mostly it has to be said when there are more undergraduates or A-level students than normal, the room can be filled with excited whispers between people who I can tell aren't really there to do any work. I can find myself looking on with great superciliousness at their lack of focus, before remembering that I too have used the room as an opportunity to scroll idly on my laptop, make whispered jokes or flirt.

Regardless of these deviations, I always feel the magic as I enter, feeling how, each day, the entrants agree to participate in the continuation of the space, asserting the importance of focused study and quiet writing. Sometimes I can't believe how many people are there, in light of the devaluing of the humanities and the collapse of many higher-education institutions, it's heartening that it is still so plentifully occupied. In this shared writer's room, suddenly I become a writer among others.

⌒

Of course, for many people, to share a space isn't at all a choice but the condition of their everyday life. When we live with family, friends, housemates or strangers, houses can be sites of immense busyness, bodies coming and going, entering and leaving. Sharing a space in this way does not have quite the same allure of the library or the cafe; instead, it can be characterised by a kind of claustrophobia, in which other people are both a real and imagined impediment to creativity. When houses contain many people and more demands, finding places and moments in which one can be creative – or at least feel free to be creative – becomes difficult. And perhaps sometimes impossible.

In the literature of mid-twentieth-century London, bedsits and boarding houses reigned, as all kinds of people, the young who had newly left home, recent arrivals from other countries and older retired singletons made little rooms in large houses their homes. Celebrated writers including Muriel Spark, Sam Selvon and Doris Lessing all took these shared living spaces as a site of dramas in their novels, contrasting the feelings of looking for a home with the idea of being inextricably involved with the lives of others. In being away from family, many young women, including some of the characters of Spark's novels *A Far Cry from Kensington* and *The Girls of Slender Means*, for example, are able to live independently, some of them working in publishing, dating and perhaps indulging in a spot of pre-marital sex. But not all the occupants of these buildings feel a sense of freedom: George Orwell's unhappy poet Gordon Comstock, of *Keep the Aspidistra Flying*, is one of those residing in close quarters with strangers. Obsessed with money, he despairs of those who have allowed their lives to be ruled by what he refers to as 'the money god' and who live comfortably as a result, symbolised in his loathed aspidistra plant, for him the ultimate representation of middle-class monotony. Having had one slim volume of poetry published, he remains stuck on a follow-up, working intermittently on his poem 'London Pleasures', a long luxuriant work, the kind that 'should only be undertaken by people with endless leisure'.[1] At the opening of the novel, Gordon lives in a shabby boarding house, shared with several other bachelors, mostly salesmen, and run by a strict landlady who keeps watch on Gordon's every move, even reading his letters. His room is chilly and sparsely furnished. After winning his landlady's approval, Gordon uses a repurposed kitchen table as a writing desk, across which lie papers and drafts that have piled up over two years; he finds that after his shift at a second-hand bookshop on poor wages, he simply can't maintain the motivation to work on his writing: 'Lack of money means discomfort, means squalid worries, means shortage of tobacco, means ever-present consciousness of failure – above all, it means loneliness.'[2] Alone in his room, he is not afforded a productive solitude, but something much bleaker, in the form of a horrible isolation from everyone around him.

Gordon is also simultaneously haunted by a different kind of writing life in the figure of a specific person, his friend and the editor of the left-wing magazine *Antichrist*, the well-meaning Ravelston. Ravelston's comfortable set-up and assured income prove a constant source of pain for Gordon, who both resents and admires him, never able to see beyond his glow of security. More gallingly, Ravelston lives alone in a comfortable flat (a pokier one than his income actually allows for), and is looked after by a housekeeper, with his offices beneath. Ravelston's private living and working spaces are everything that Gordon does not have.

These kinds of boarding-house living arrangements are nowhere near as common as they were in the decades between the 1920s and 1970s. Yet, in 2025, the UK is immured in a housing crisis, one that takes many shapes and forms: not only is there a lack of affordable housing for young people and those on lower incomes, but living standards have been on the decline for those renting, and tenants live with the unsettling threat of so-called 'no fault' evictions. Most shockingly, there has also been a huge jump in homelessness – according to the homeless charity Shelter, there was an increase of 14 per cent between 2023 and 2024.[3] Taken together, it is obvious that for an ever-greater number of people, the idea of home as a safe place is completely out of reach; how is anyone to be creative in a precarious space that does not feel like theirs, and may even feel in some way to reject them?

Rather than finding those spaces of 'one's own', young adults are sharing houses either with housemates or with family for longer than previous generations – living in a kind of arrested youth. Newspapers talk dismissively of the reliance of millennials on 'the Bank of Mum and Dad' (a report from 2019 suggested that parents have become the sixth biggest money lender in the UK[4]), conveniently forgetting why that might be – the 2008 crash, subsequent austerity politics across Europe and the US, the increasing precarity and 'uberisation' of work. People who are able to buy a home in their twenties and thirties nearly always rely on help from their parents in one way or another, to give them the deposit, to take out another mortgage on their own home, or purchase the house outright. The route to homeowning can be a protracted affair, not necessarily the result of 'hard work' (whatever that means) or years of saving, but the intermingling of employment prospects, luck and the benefits that come from the relative ease of earlier generations.

This precariousness and uncertainty impacts on the way that people understand the relationship between work and life, between writing and money. For working-class writers, writing can feel risky, even dangerous, a distraction from the promised safety and security of better-paid jobs with legible career paths. The possibility of writing as a profession can feel so distant as to seem completely unrelated to 'real' work. Novelist Kit de Waal has been an important advocate for working-class voices in publishing and has spoken about beginning to write in her forties while caring for her children after years of working in family law. In her life, she notes in one piece, 'No one from my background – poor, black and Irish – wrote books. It just wasn't an option.'[5] For others, setting out on a career in writing doesn't mean retreating to a comfortable work space, but carving out time when and where you can in places that may feel unreceptive, maybe even hostile. Novelist Michael Magee writes of balancing writing against the physical burden of insecure service work, feeling at the whim of a scary landlord from whom he rents a small room in a shared house, noting, 'It's difficult to maintain a creative output when you're not sure how long the situation is going to last.'[6] In these accounts, the romance of the writer's room has all but disappeared; none of these writers spend time detailing their desks, their writing implements, their routines: the focus is on simply getting the writing done.

Writing and publishing more generally cannot shake its relationship to middle-class life, not least because the median income of a writer has fallen so staggeringly – an Authors' Licensing and Collecting Society (ALCS) report records a decline of 38.2 per cent between 2018 and 2022.[7] The danger becomes, as many writers have pointed out, that writing is done only by those who already have security in other aspects of their lives and have rooms of their own (or other people's) that they can fall back on. For the writer Daisy Lafarge, she can't help but wonder, 'What if I were the kind of writer whose parents bought them a flat in London, or one who was able to better focus on writing because the precarity of renting was only a temporary prelude to the balm of inheritance?'[8] In Lafarge's view, the possibility of secure living suggests a totally different relationship with writing, where her work would not be conceived of in terms of the rent for which it pays. She wonders if the removal of the psychic noise of worry would improve her writing – writing that isn't rushed, isn't hurried, isn't precarious. This is a hard question to answer, something we can't know for certain, but it seems not too far-fetched to imagine that writers like the twentieth-century poet Edith Sitwell, with her esoteric writing and idiosyncratic personality and style, could produce what they did only because they were cushioned by large estates.

This worry about what creativity can happen at home makes spaces such as libraries all the more important. Libraries offer not only the promise of shared resources, books to borrow, computers to use, or desks to sit at, but also a shared purpose. In entering the building of the British Library, I become enmeshed in a history of learning, reading and writing, in a place both relatively new and impossibly old, finding a sense of possibility in simply being around others.

This iteration of the library, situated on the Euston Road, noisy with traffic and hazy with pollution, is only its most recent form, opened in 1997. The original library was situated further into Bloomsbury, when the layout of the area was open and green, housed in the refurbished mansion Montagu House. The concept of a 'British Library' emerged in 1753, as part of the British Museum Act, which, among other things, sought to establish a 'national library'.[9] Montagu House had been previously destroyed in a fire, so to open its doors as the library it was extensively refurbished, finally opening in 1759 with an announcement of its free entry to all 'studious and curious persons'. The British Museum Act did not just cover the building, but the contents of the library too: the basis of its collections were the papers and objects of individuals who had built up extensive archives that ran from the historical to the biblical, and even precious stones. In the far-reaching aims of the act, the British government founded the museum as well as working to acquire its specific identity, collecting material and, therefore, knowledge, crafting an idea of 'Britishness', one that could be disseminated both at home and abroad – an idea often based on objects taken from other countries.

This idea of shoring up and collecting knowledge was something Virginia Woolf thought about as she continued her investigations into the cultural 'poverty' of women in *A Room of One's Own*. In the iconic round Reading Room of the British Museum, now closed, watching the students around her make copious notes while deep in concentration, the narrator of *Room* finds that her pencil stays still. As she examines her surroundings, she feels a deep anger growing at the person she calls 'the professor', the writer who produces the books that line the shelves around her, books that see women as an object to be studied. The 'professor' is also the judge, the company director, the editor, standing in for the whole patriarchy, an exclusionary and angry figure, and fashioned on perpetuating the idea of the superiority of men over women.[10] In this place of shared industry, Woolf's narrator cannot find her place, not through lack of effort but because of the exclusion the space represents. It might be shared, but in this room she is an object, not a creator.

When the round Reading Room that Woolf writes about was opened in 1857, it was the culmination of the radical principles of the Keeper of Printed Books, Antonio Panizzi. Though the original intention had been, as the library's announcement in 1759 suggested, for the library to be free to 'studious and curious persons', what that meant in practice was quite different. Historian Ruth Hoberman found that, in the first ten years after the museum opened, 'only three women used it',[11] and that later into the nineteenth century a taboo on women reading in public still remained, with middle-class women more likely to prefer reading books at home. Nevertheless, the anxiety about who went into the room was not limited to women; Panizzi's push to rethink the reading room came from his desire to open the collections to more than gentlemen, commenting in a select committee meeting in 1836, 'I want a poor student to have the same means of indulging his learned curiosity, of following his rational pursuits, of consulting the same authorities, of fathoming the most intricate inquiry, as the richest man in the kingdom.'[12] This access would mean more funding from the government, better organisation of the catalogues, and the expansion of the kinds of material that made up the collection. In other words, it meant effort and attention, and an acknowledgement that the space was closed off to some in the first place.

Though the collections were indeed made more accessible, and have since wildly expanded to a dizzying number of books, journals, newspapers, magazines, and with a much larger number of reading rooms, an interested visitor who wants to use any of these resources still has to prove themselves for entry. To apply for a Reader card, one needs documentation, proof of address, a picture taken. I see unknowing visitors try to enter the rooms only to be turned away, confused and unsure about why they aren't able to take a peek or borrow something. But this is the tension of the British Library, between a place to visit and a place to study. This pull of focus existed even in the early days when it was still the British Museum, between those who wanted to consult the collections and those who wanted to visit the antiquities.[13] Though the building is a public building, in the most obvious sense of the word, created for people to use, it doesn't have the same function as a local library, where you are able to borrow books alongside singing and story sessions for children. Yet I find myself marvelling at how many people pass through its doors each day who are not there to study, but instead to glean something about reading, or perhaps about London. Some, no doubt, arrive with a similar intention to those who go to writer's house museums – to gaze upon some revered objects of the past, a Shakespeare first folio or copy of Magna Carta in the Treasures collection. Evidence of the building's connection to the past is everywhere: in the centre of the building stands a tall atrium in which many of the oldest books of the library are stored. They remain, in their aged glory, resting behind the glass like Woolf's desk or Carlyle's manuscripts, the titles on their spines often undecipherable, yet tantalising. When tour guides lead around excited tourists and serious retirees, they stop and describe the way these manuscripts and folios have been collected, deposited, though truth be told I have never listened closely. To me they feel like decoration rather than historical items, an addition to the building to illustrate its history, without actually revealing anything substantial. These strange parallel purposes, the confident strides of those who know the building well versus the tentative steps of someone entering for the first time, reveal the complexity of sharing a building quite so unique.

Not everyone has the time freedom or support to undertake the work the reading rooms suggest. Even more so, the space of the library can speak in a harsher voice, in entrances and exits, about who is allowed to come and to go, who is allowed in and out. Though modern libraries have many initiatives to get people from across the community inside their doors, the 'public' aspect of the public library has a more fraught history, particularly to those whom that sense of 'public' is actually addressed. James Baldwin's first novel, *Go Tell It on the Mountain*, published in 1953, tells the story of a young man growing up in Harlem, New York. At one point the young man, named John, walks around Manhattan, weaving through Central Park, down Fifth Avenue, and on to 42nd Street. His journey takes him to the location of a building he much admires, the New York Public Library, with its famous stone lions that sit solemnly either side of its staircase. But John finds that he doesn't feel able to enter, intimidated by its size; more than that, he doesn't want to be seen to be confused by its grand scale because 'then everyone, all the white people inside, would know that he was not used to great buildings, or to many books, and they would look at him with pity'.[14] Though ostensibly public, the New York Public Library is not, for this young Black man, a welcoming place, guarded by those fearsome stone lions. For John, the public world is divided into places where he is and is not able to go; he must divine, by feeling, where is the right place for him to be, where he does and does not belong. The library is a place of potential, where he may one day fit in, 'when he had read all the books uptown' that would 'lend him the poise to enter any building in the world'.[15] For some people, especially those who have been historically overtly excluded from some spaces, the ability to read, to write, to share in this knowledge, is premised on credentials they have been made to feel are out of their reach. In John's life, the building speaks in the voice of Woolf's 'professor' – forbidding and judging.

⌒

Since the birth of my son, the idea of other people has taken on an entirely new meaning, as each day I learn what it means to live with a new person, especially one as noisy and excitable as a toddler. The way I occupy the space of my house has altered irrevocably, as I take new routes from room to room to change a nappy, find clean clothes or play chase. My house is the same, and in many ways so am I, and yet I am also profoundly changed, as my time and attention is taken up with the many tasks of childrearing. In this louder, more tiring kind of living, privacy is harder to come by and I have had to recalibrate the ways in which I can be alone to think and work. Writing happens in those in-between moments, no longer at a desk but as I am slumped on a chair in the living room, or while my son naps. There are no guarantees in this new writing life about when I'll be able to do it or if, after a bad night's sleep, I'll even have the wherewithal to put my fingers to the keyboard. Unlike my co-workers of the British Library, the person I share my workspace with now cares very little for the world of writing, and is indeed happiest when I am giving him my fullest attention.

In this new way of working, I join countless other women who have wondered how they can make a creative life for themselves while also having children. Critic Alexandra Schwartz summarises this conflict: 'A mother must make herself always available. A writer needs to shut the door.'[16] Is the home capacious enough to contain so many simultaneous versions of living? The home itself has never been a stable category either – what we do in it and how we think about it has changed over hundreds of years. But even over these shifting times, women have often been made synonymous with domesticity, finding our place within it feeling at odds with the possibilities of its confinement. Even in the early days of feminist writing, women considered the home as a vehicle through which the rules that governed their lives were enforced. Charlotte Perkins Gilman famously wrote in her story *The Yellow Wallpaper* about the restriction of a woman to a single room after childbirth, and her descent into a kind of overwhelming madness.

The narrator's husband, a doctor, insists she spends most of her time in a room at the top of their house – fittingly, a nursery – and forbids her to write, insisting that she have 'perfect rest'.[17] She does manage to sneak some writing time, but in secret, while her husband is away on his rounds and she is alone. The reader never gets a sense of why exactly the narrator writes, but the husband's ban on it ('he hates to have me write a word'[18]) suggests its importance. As she finds herself becoming increasingly disturbed and fixated on the patterns on the wallpaper of the nursery, and the woman she sees trapped within it, her writing evidences the damage that this extended rest cure is inflicting on her. The nursery becomes a writing room by stealth but also out of necessity.

Feminist philosopher Simone de Beauvoir, whose work *The Second Sex* was a crucial text for the burgeoning movement of feminism that was to follow, wrote about the house as a site of continual labour for those women tasked, most often solo, with its maintenance: 'Few tasks are more similar to the torment of Sisyphus than those of the housewife, day after day, one must wash dishes, dust furniture, mend clothes that will be dirty, dusty and torn again. The housewife wears herself out running on the spot; she does nothing; she only perpetuates the present.'[19] As Beauvoir finds, the upkeep of the home becomes a way of living in an everlasting *now*: how is one to plan, to think, and to create anew and project forwards when tasked with such an enormous load of repetitive work? American artist Martha Rosler's piece from 1975, *Semiotics of the Kitchen*, is one of the most famous pieces of feminist art from this period: a woman stands facing the camera (the artist herself) and, in a deadpan voice, names and demonstrates the use of each tool of the kitchen, both parodying increasingly popular cookery shows and undermining any notion of creativity and self-expression in that space. For feminist writers, the burden of the (albeit shared) home fell to the woman alone; the lonely arduousness of this eradicated any space for anything else.

Rachel Cusk was widely disparaged in the aftermath of her publication *A Life's Work* in 2001, her memoir about pregnancy and motherhood, not only because of her frank discussions of the boredom and monotony of sharing space and life with a baby, but also because she examines the enormous upheaval of a child on her identity: 'I have given up my membership of the world I used to live in.'[20] Not only do women feel differently after having a child, but women are *seen* differently too. Roland Barthes noticed the entrenchment of this split in the way that women writers were written about in French fashion magazine *Elle* during the 1950s; he saw that regardless of the subject of their writing, the world around them would always bring them back to their domestic lives, the 'other' life they live with their children: 'Let us tie the adventure of art to the strong pillars of the home.'[21] A few years later, British writer Margaret Drabble famously included a scene in her important 1960 novel *The Millstone* in which a baby literally eats the pages of a book manuscript.

Perhaps it is unsurprising that so many of the women whose work has made it into the 'canon' of great writers were childless. In fact, feminist and writer Tillie Olsen notices that the women who have become assimilated into that select list have several factors in common in their rejection of heteronormativity, whether that be in having children or in getting married. By avoiding, or sometimes delaying, those 'milestones' traditionally laid out for women, this small coterie could enter into the supposedly 'man's world' of writing. Olsen also finds that even those women, such as Emily Dickinson, who seemingly eschewed the responsibilities of family by staying single for the duration of their lives, had help in the home in the form of servants who provided so much additional support.

Years before Tillie Olsen, Virginia Woolf also noticed the childlessness of some of the women whose work was the basis of her analysis of *A Room of One's Own*,[22] something she felt very conflicted about in her own life. At the same time, Woolf finds that there is indeed a history of women's writing in Britain, as she charts the careers of people such as Margaret Cavendish and

Aphra Behn, two of the best-known women writers of the eighteenth century, discovering that it was indeed possible for women in that century to begin to write for money. This is confirmed, though very casually, in the scholar Ian Watt's famous *The Rise of the Novel* from 1957, a book that documents the establishing of the novel form and a stalwart of literature degrees across the country. In among his discussions of Samuel Richardson and Daniel Defoe, Watt does acknowledge that the majority of the writing published in the eighteenth century was by women, without naming any writers or specific texts; the suggestion being that though women were doing the writing, what they were producing wasn't 'really' literature, and maybe even wasn't 'real' writing.[23] Regardless of the way the work is judged now, it evidences that some women were indeed finding time to write, it just didn't look the same or enjoy the same lasting reputation. As Woolf writes, 'Anon, who wrote so many poems without signing them, was often a woman.'[24] The canon of literature that is remembered to this day, partially constructed by studies like Watt's, is another version of Woolf's experience of the round Reading Room, a space of exclusion.

Women have always found ways to express themselves, in among the textures of the day, even if it means having to rethink the bare bones of where that can take place. In the 1970s, the feminist writer Alta Gerrey published a slim volume about her life as a mother examining with brutal honesty her experience of raising her two daughters, her relationships and moments of failure. Even when she is exhausted, and struggling to keep her temper or earn enough money, she carves out moments to create, finding that the space she can use in her house is determined by other people, not only her children, but visitors too. For a time, her writing room was her front room: '(where else would a woman write? how else could she watch the kids out the window while being immortal on paper? or how else could she hear the water boil? huh?)'.[25] Alta has no formal space that is hers alone and when she does write she has to be flexible and, more often than not, share it with her children – she cannot separate out these parts of herself. She explains that writing happens in 'snatch[ed] quiet moments' perhaps even as other things need to get done, 'applying bandages, rinsing out bottles, wiping bottoms, picking scraps of paper off the floor, answering telephones, fixing food, & stopping quarrels'.[26] Tillie Olsen finds that working in this way changes not just the way you live but the way you think: 'habits of years – response to others, distractibility, responsibility for daily matters – stay with you, mark you, become you . . . what should take weeks takes me sometimes months to write; what should take months, takes years'.[27] This is another transformation of time, keeping women in a continuous present, as Beauvoir found, and stretching out the time that is there. Writing work has to happen at the same time as so much other, non-creative, activity.

Of course, writing with family is not only something that affects women, but men too. When in 1964 J. G. Ballard's wife Mary died suddenly while the family was on holiday in Spain, the writer was left to raise their three children alone. In the mid-sixties Ballard was already writing solidly, but it was in the following years that he produced his famous and controversial works, *The Atrocity Exhibition* (1970) and *Crash* (1973), while also looking after his family. For Ballard, that work of care was his priority, and so his writing happened, with a surprising ease, 'between ironing a school tie, serving up the sausage and mash, and watching *Blue Peter*'.[28] Echoing the words of Cyril Connolly, Ballard welcomed the distractions the 'pram in the hall' brought to his life, and throughout his memoir *Miracles of Life* he writes with deep love and admiration for the children he clearly worked hard to bring up. His daughter Bea explains how intertwined their family life was with Ballard's work schedule:

> By day we had a pact and would leave him alone for a few hours, but we could not resist slipping through his door to ask questions. He would be in the middle of composing a sentence, mouthing out the words as he wrote. Sometimes

he would tell us about the book he was writing and ask us to name the characters, handing us the telephone directory with the instruction: 'Think of a good name for a doctor...'[29]

It's hard not to admire his commitment to his family as well as his work ethic. At the same time, he gives an insight elsewhere about other aspects of the Ballard home that fell by the wayside: 'most of the women who know me would say I made a very slatternly mother, notably unkeen on housework, unaware that homes need to be cleaned now and then, and too often found with a cigarette in one hand and a drink in the other'.[30] Ballard's time as mother and father was not totally under the thumb of all those pressures that women so often face, namely the keeping of the house as well as the children. For many women, these two things are expected to go hand in hand: in Alta's writing, for example, she becomes distracted by the dirty window under which her desk sits, so much so that she is compelled to get up and clean it. She considers how this moment in her writing might be discussed by a professor in a university classroom, a situation where the window would, in her mind, always be considered as a vehicle for other loftier meanings. But Alta brings it back down to the most practical: 'it aint no metaphor, teach. i just got up & washed the fuckin window.'[31] Where Ballard finds writing in among family remarkably straightforward, for many women, the labour of the house itself unavoidable provides the material that becomes the topic of that very writing.

I know, in talking to female friends over the years, that housework can cause friction and upset in even the most equal-seeming relationships. At the same time, homes are far more complicated than simply sites of labour: we spend our lives in our homes, and we find ways of making them joyful too. As feminist sociologist Iris Marion Young puts it, 'Not all homemaking is housework.'[32] My friend Susanna has a marvellous way of filling each space she lives in with personal touches – photos, dried flowers, wreaths – and I'm proud that visitors have always complimented my husband and me on the sense of cosiness we manage to create. This homemaking is echoed in the work of other writers who have made the home and the activities that define it a crucial part of their creative practice. The writer and illustrator Judith Kerr found her family home in Barnes, London, the perfect setting for the entirety of her writing life; she speaks with great affection for the way that it facilitated not only her own work but her husband's, the writer Thomas Nigel Kneale, their workrooms companionably side by side, allowing for shared lunch and tea breaks; here they worked until Thomas's death in 2006. 'It's awfully like coming home, up here,' she tells interviewer Candice Pires in 2017, later adding, 'It's the place where I know where I am, now Tom has gone.'[33]

Kerr's inspiration didn't take place only in the house, but looked to objects of the home too: the family really did have a cat called Mog, who would later inspire a whole series of books, and the family kitchen was a backdrop to many of her stories, including *The Tiger Who Came to Tea*. She noted simply that she included the kitchen units in her work because they were 'what we had'.[34] I wonder, though, if their presence was a way of communicating the centrality of the kitchen in her life with Thomas and their two children. Kerr's engagement with the detail of her own space is a different way of imagining its boundaries, not as a way of closing off inspiration, but as actively facilitating it, acknowledging that our shared homes have as much right to be included in our writing as anything else.

In 2022, The National Centre for Children's Books in Newcastle acquired some of these units, distinctive in their mid-century design and colour palette of yellow and white. The kitchen was offered to the centre by Kerr's estate after the Barnes property she had lived in for so long was being refitted; a few of the units now sit nestled in a corner of one of the centre's rooms, with onions hung from a hook and a tea pot and cups set out ready to welcome a thirsty guest or two. Though the scene is behind glass, it still remains strangely inconspicuous, especially as it sits in contrast to a very large stuffed tiger who looms at a table nearby, surrounded by play food, awaiting little visitors to re-enact the story. Kerr's kitchen is a very different kind of preserved writer's space, hinting at the sprawl of creative life, spilling out far beyond the confines of a single room.

The American writer Ursula Le Guin, who wrote many of her famous works while raising three children, commented that keeping house and caring for them were part of what she calls simply 'stupid ordinary stuff',[35] crucial for keeping her tethered and connected to the 'real world' outside writing. For some writers there never seemed to be quite the same sense of opposition, the object of the kitchen table itself acting as a facilitator, even reframing crucial ideas about creative life itself. The founders of Kitchen Table: Women of Color Press, which included writers and feminists Audre Lorde, Barbara Smith and Cherríe Moraga, wanted to create a way that they could publish their work and the work of other writers while circumventing traditional publishing routes. Giving an account of the press's aims and intentions in the late 1980s, Smith explains that it came out of the acknowledgement that publishing needed more diverse avenues of publication to ensure that voices such as hers and her co-founders could be heard. To represent this, the founders envisioned the kitchen table as an alternative locus of invention. Rather than the secluded, quiet and private space of the writer's room, they turned their attention to the noisy, bustling and, most importantly, feminised space of the home. For Smith, the name has a double resonance, not only because the kitchen table is 'the place where women in particular work and communicate with each other' but also because it evokes their very approach, the fact of being 'a kitchen table, grass-roots operation, begun and kept alive by women who cannot rely on inheritances or other benefits of class privilege to do the work we need to do'.[36] Smith invokes the kitchen table in its significance as a place of both talk and labour, as well as a metaphor for the way that some poor women and women of colour had to make their own opportunities. In this we see that the press was trying to challenge not only the way that work is made, but how it is disseminated, and perhaps how work could be made in the future.

Smith and her collaborators were not the only writers specifically invoking the shared kitchen table as a way of rethinking what creativity looks like and, indeed, what the writer's room can be; the American writer Paule Marshall writes of her experience growing up listening to the discussions of her mother and friends at various kitchen tables in the brownstones of Brooklyn, finding that the ranging subjects, jokey tones and play with language was her first taste of writing. She saw herself as growing up 'among poets' even if 'they didn't look like poets – whatever that breed is supposed to look like'.[37] These 'unknown bards' as she calls them worked as cleaners and housekeepers, normally for white women, and were paid poorly for their efforts; in their free time the women would come together at the kitchen table to talk, and in their talk produce a kind of shared poetry. Marshall describes listening in as she and her sister sat nearby doing homework, and finding that her mother and friends would come alive in these conversations. Though there was also gossip and chit-chat, in getting together to exchange words and ideas the women could play with language, and find ways to be creative in their day-to-day lives. She saw how it was possible to make talk into an 'art form that – in keeping with the African tradition in which art and life are one – was an integral part of their lives'.[38] In the example of these women, creativity looks very different: not only a collective endeavour, full of energy, but made by people who weren't picking up a pen.

In a very different home around a hundred years earlier was another scene of joint enterprise, taking place among the Brontë siblings. Charlotte, Emily, Anne and their brother Branwell started creating work as children, writing plays and later inventing whole fictional worlds with extensive lore. These siblings were very close, even more so after the death of their mother in 1821, followed not long after by their two sisters Maria and Elizabeth. The novelist

Elizabeth Gaskell was a close friend of Charlotte Brontë, and after her death wrote her biography. In a description of the early life of Charlotte and the other Brontës, Gaskell describes their serious approach to learning and reading from a tender age, reflected in the layout of the parsonage in Haworth that they grew up in: 'This little extra upstairs room was appropriated to the children. Small as it was, it was not called a nursery; indeed, it had not the comfort of a fire-place in it; the servants . . . called the room the "children's study".'[39] These studious children became industrious young people, not only in their working lives (the Brontës had to find employment) but also on their own creative projects, oftentimes writing side by side. Gaskell describes a typical scene:

> The sisters retained the old habit, which was begun in their aunt's life-time, of putting away their work at nine o'clock, and beginning their study, pacing up and down the sitting room. At this time, they talked over the stories they were engaged upon, and described their plots. Once or twice a week, each read to the others what she had written, and heard what they had to say about it.[40]

This collective creation came through conversation but also companionship: work that took place while in touching distance with siblings. We see how close in a sketch from Emily's diary in June 1837, in which she and her sister Anne are sitting together, at work at the family's dining-room table. With papers strewn across its surface, this is a scene of happy and shared industry.

Sometimes, we end up in shared spaces we could never have imagined, spaces that are horribly exposing, even unpleasant. In these times we can feel trapped and claustrophobic, the presence of other people an invasion rather than a comfort. Dennis Potter's TV drama *The Singing Detective* is set in one such place, a large Victorian hospital ward filled with male patients suffering from long-term conditions or recovering from a procedure. Philip Marlow, his name a reference to the famous Raymond Chandler character, is not a detective himself, but a writer of detective stories, and is suffering from an acute flare-up of psoriatic arthritis, an incredibly painful condition that affects both the skin and the joints – something Potter himself experienced. As Marlow lies in his narrow bed, bored and profoundly depressed, he falls into a strange dream world, between memory and fantasy. Having previously suffered from writer's block, and not having worked for several years, Marlow, trapped in his bed, and for much of the series, trapped in his head, finds he is motivated to write once more, but is prohibited from physically doing it. The hustle and bustle of the ward, filled with other patients and the coming and goings of the nurses and the porters, is not conducive to the way we might imagine the work of writing to be and yet Marlow always drifts back, rewriting himself as the star of his own novel, *The Singing Detective*, or cutting together scenes from memory, re-examining his childhood. Though Marlow is severely physically limited due to his condition, we are privy to the narratives he is constructing internally, enabling him to write for us without him ever having to touch the page.

As I watched this show, marvelling at Dennis Potter's ability to reframe the detective story into something truly profound, I thought about the way that Marlow's investigations, both his delving into his troubled past and within the detective story he is weaving, gave a sense of the creative possibility of any space. Or, to put it another way, that even the most unlikely of spaces can allow for, or even enable, work to happen. Towards the end of the first episode, Marlow sits in his hospital bed in a daze, plotting the detective story we have just been watching, when a doctor interrupts him – one of the many seemingly well-meaning but deeply patronising members of staff that Marlow encounters there. Marlow is quick to explain his impatience at the constant interruptions he endures: 'I am trying to do some work . . . or are you one of the great majority who thinks that writing isn't work? . . . Or do you by any chance labour under the delusion that it consists solely and entirely of actually putting words on the page, without thought, without planning, as if I were a *Sunday Times* journalist or something?'[41] Marlow asserts the right for his work to be taken seriously, even if he is in deep despair, and even if he cannot grasp a pen – and indeed he isn't able to until much later in the series. But the doctor is not listening, in fact, none of the doctors who treat Marlow seem to be, and instead chastise him for his anger and fear in the face of pain. The only thing that keeps him going is the freedom afforded by the writing he does in his head.

Anyone who has been in a waiting room or a hospital ward knows that these spaces transform our sense of self. Here we become a patient, made of numbers waiting to be measured and recorded, or a diagnosis ready to be written out in the messy hand of the doctor, or typed up on a form. In the aftermath of a complicated miscarriage, I did a lot of waiting in waiting rooms. Each time I made the trip to my local hospital, a short walk from my house, to get my blood drawn to check my hormone levels, I wondered if I should be ready with words to record my feelings. On a few occasions I brought a notebook with me, in the hope that I could make the waiting room into a writing room, even for a few moments. But the space paralysed me in its awfulness; I didn't want to think about the words that might bring myself onto the page; I wanted to be anywhere else. Each return to the waiting room brought confrontation with the suffering of other women going through some version of what I was emerging from. I brought old copies of the *London Review of Books*, thinking I could distract myself out of despair with reading the words of those cleverer and more certain than me. In the end, I mostly watched whatever was on the television that hung in the corner of the room: episodes of *The Simpsons* or *A Place in the Sun*.

But even in those very toughest moments, sometimes writing and the urge to write can overtake. In December 2022, while watching television with his partner in Rome, the British writer Hanif Kureishi, known for his many novels including *My Beautiful Laundrette* and *The Buddha of Suburbia*, suddenly collapsed, which subsequently led to almost full-body paralysis. Not long after, as Kureishi began to understand the long-term impact the accident would have, he started publishing with great frequency on Substack, collecting what he called 'dispatches from my hospital bed'. I followed this writing, amazed at how much he was putting down, and how often. Remarkably, Kureishi records not only his experiences, the profoundly difficult and painful realisations he has made about the capabilities of the body, but also about writing itself. In fact, many of the dispatches are not really about his accident or its legacy at all, but about how and why we write. His son Carlo commented in an interview not long after the accident: 'He's writing more than he's written in years. He's writing 1,000 words a day, which is incredible considering his condition. And he's really got a subject now to talk about, which is always what a writer needs.'[42]

But Kureishi, like Marlow, cannot hold a pen in his writing hand or put fingers to a keyboard. What I and many others were reading, produced so thoughtfully and frequently, was formed through new collaborative relationships with his partner Isabella and his sons: they discuss, he dictates, and a loved one types. For Kureishi, this way of working completely altered not only how the writing itself was made, but its very essence, as he comments in one Substack: 'I'm not sure that I'd like to go back to working solo again after this experiment, which has sparked a new creative era for me.'[43] In another post, Hanif and Carlo talk about the way they put together their pieces, Carlo marvelling at the speed at which the two of them work, Hanif on how his son both inspires the pieces they create and how diligently he edits. Hanif says at one point:

> When I'm writing alone, I go dead sometimes, feeling worthless. But, because you and I are here for a fixed time, and these meetings mean so much to me in my present,

physical state, I cannot let myself go dead. You help keep my desire to write alive. Our collaboration has altered the quantity and quality of my writing.[44]

Kureishi is enlivened by the presence of his son; in the reframing of writing not as a something one must do as a lone endeavour but produced in tandem with another, enhanced, in fact, by the presence of those other people. The interaction between them is beautiful, and shows just how tender and transformative collaboration in shared spaces – both physically and online – can be.

While this new way of working came from an emergency, for some writers sharing a space is and has always been a crucial part of their process. Where I have relied on the British Library, for many others it is the company of a select few. Writer Rebecca Schiller set up her Mothers Who Write network to support writers who happen to be mothers to find ways of claiming space for themselves, and arranges both in-person retreats as well as Zoom writing sessions. The London Writers' Salon hosts four single writing hours each day, one for each major time zone: anyone can join, all they need is the intention to write. This is something I have set up for myself too, working not with strangers but my friend Laura, an academic, who like me has a book to finish. Over the course of a few months, we arrange various online meetings, me in London, her in Sheffield. We have a little routine, starting each session with a brief chat, talking about what we've been doing these last few days, and then get to work, she on her book, and I mine. I keep the Teams screen up next to my Word document, hoping some of her serious focus can transmit to me through the pixels. I've found during these short hours that I am always more productive than I had felt able to be even moments before I clicked 'Join'. For me, and all those other writers who share online spaces, we ask for more than accountability from one another; we invite each other into our homes or indeed a myriad of other places, creating a new kind of writing room between us. When you don't have the time or luxury of being 'blocked', these virtual meetings allow for work simply to get *done*. In these virtual rooms, writing becomes a shared activity, something that happens because of the participation of other people, not in spite of them.

In truth, other people have always been in writing rooms, or sitting alongside our writers. Yet their presence has so often been obscured, reaffirming the existence of the solitary genius. Many great works of literature have been hashed out with friends or partners, whether in writer's salons or in bedrooms; many other works were dictated to someone else who diligently scribbled or typed, the 'invisible hands' as scholars Leah Price and Pamela Thurschwell put it, that were more often than not women. Writing and producing creative work has always entailed sharing space, whether we acknowledge it or not. Living in a shared house, the writer Amber Medland finds that the possibility of other people becomes part of the landscape of writing, motivating her to work in the time before their arrival home after their own work elsewhere, and providing a supportive ear once they come through the door. More practically, 'Being able to hear people talking constantly is good training for writing dialogue.'[45] Like Ursula Le Guin, Medland finds creative value in a life that is interwoven with others.

Living among others, our family, friends and strangers, is hard, but it is also the stuff that makes our life meaningful and worthwhile. I'm struck by the image of the American writer Kate Zambreno breastfeeding her daughter while balancing a laptop on her knees, or of Buchi Emecheta's main character Adah, in her novel *Second Class Citizen*, scribbling down her novel as she too nurses her newborn; in fact, Emecheta herself dedicates that book to her own children, writing 'without whose sweet background noises this book would not have been written'.[46] Emecheta's loving words to her brood quietly reject those assumptions about the writer's room, envisioning instead a space exuberantly populated, not keeping other people out but welcoming them in.

The writer's cafe: Hucks, London, May 2025.

Chapter 4

TEMPORARY SPACES

This book has taken me far beyond the desk. Though I dreamed the perfect item of furniture would anchor me in my identity as a writer, I have found that my writing life is defined not by one space, but several. In fact, more and more of my writing has been done in ways I couldn't have predicted, sometimes scribbled hastily in a tatty notebook as I wait for a coffee, or recorded as voice notes on my phone as I pace up and down the platform of the train station waiting to make my way back to London after a busy day of teaching. I've been at home, certainly, allowing the paint of my white desk to get increasingly grubby and messy, books and notes piling higher and higher and, of course, much of the past few years has been shaped by the space and people of the

British Library, by the potential for elements there to impinge, to distract, and to alter. But my writing has also become haphazard and changeable, and in some moments not at all rooted to the space I'm in. I've found that staying put can sometimes feel too stolid; what I've needed instead is movement, a kinetic feeling of ideas emerging, becoming more vivid, almost in tandem with my footsteps.

As I've looked further into the writer's room, it's obvious that for many of the individuals who make up my cast of writers, different places have served them at different moments too, and the possibility of writing in spaces that are defined by their temporariness is appealing, often crucial. Sometimes the spaces created in a house just don't pass muster; as Virginia Woolf wrote in her diary in January 1930, 'I cannot write naturally in my new room, because the table is not the right height and I must stoop to warm my hands.'[1] Her sense of the space's inadequacy led her to look outside her room and to create her writing lodge. But this was a permanent shift, a recasting of her scene of writing. For other women, those who have not had the same material comforts and security, writing has had to work differently, even being characterised by the reality of the temporary space, whether finding places in the home as we saw in the example of Alta, or further afield. Theorist and activist Gloria E. Anzaldúa looks both near and far, writing that one must 'forget the room of one's own – write in the kitchen, lock yourself up in the bathroom. Write on the bus or the welfare line, on the job or during meals, between sleeping or waking. I write while sitting on the john.'² Anzaldúa imagines here, quite beautifully, an unceasing creativity, words that need an outlet regardless of the place in which they emerge, occurring because of their uncomfortable and cramped conditions, in the strange moments after waking, and even on the toilet. Tillie Olsen writes of this too: 'Time on the bus, even when I had to stand, was enough; the stolen moments at work, enough; the deep night hours for as long as I could stay awake, after the kids were in bed, after the household tasks were done, sometimes during.'³ For both writers, these methods may have been the only way for them to be able to work at all, but they hold another power too: those small in-between instants come to characterise the process of thinking, a way of giving space and shape to thought. The writer Audre Lorde found exactly that, choosing to write poems because 'of all the art forms, poetry is the most economical . . . requires the least physical labour, the least material, and the one which can be done between shifts, in the hospital pantry, on the subway, and on scraps of surplus paper.'⁴ For Lorde, there is something in the very essence of poetry itself, its compression, its precision, that lends itself to the shifting nature of writing that happens in among living. Like Emily Dickinson's writing on the edges of recipes and on the backs of letters, Lorde's poetry emerged from the very materials of life, the 'scraps of surplus paper' we collect as we go about our daily routines.

Selma James, the feminist and activist who co-founded the International Wages for Housework movement in the 1970s, saw that in order for her to attend properly to her writing, she had to leave her house altogether. At the instigation of C. L. R. James, the great Marxist scholar and later Selma's husband, she used a compositional method of his design, writing down ideas as and when they came to her and putting them in a shoebox. From these scraps, she shaped what would eventually become the essay, 'A Woman's Place'. As James explains in her introduction to the piece, she knew that if she 'stayed home from work to put the draft together, I would end up cleaning the oven or doing some other major piece of housework'. So she arranged to spend the day at a friend's house instead: 'I left home at the same time as I would have if I'd gone to work, dropped my son at the nursery, and arrived at my friend's at 8 a.m., just as she was leaving for work. The house was empty. I had no distractions or excuses ... by six or seven that evening, I had the draft of a pamphlet.'[5] At the point of writing, James was living in Brooklyn and had a job in a factory alongside looking after a young son; her life was overwhelmed by those two modes of being and, in the space of her home, there was no room for a third. Seeking out this *other* home, where she was not its keeper but a guest, allowed for those responsibilities to fall away for a time. Unlike the shared domestic spaces we encountered previously, here James's writing space is characterised by its very temporariness, and by the sense of relief that brings. To be outside her own space, one she feels makes certain demands on her and her behaviours, allows her a neutrality, a safety from an overwhelming mental load.

I am lucky in that I can return to a home where I do not feel alone in its maintenance, and where I feel safe and loved, but that doesn't mean that I don't often have the desire to find a spot that allows me, even for a few hours, to be something else. I put myself together and step out of my door with a sense of possibility: in being on the move, I can delve into new feelings, new ideas that come specifically from the not-being in place. Taking a simple walk can help loosen what felt tightly wound, can allow some half-formed idea to take shape, even redirect a whole chapter. Much of my PhD was written while stomping around the streets of Bloomsbury, worrying, brooding, but ultimately finding answers.

Some of these walks have led me to the space of the cafe, where I look not for the feeling of being on the move, but to be hosted for a while by strangers. In the shared space of the cafe, I am joined by some who unite with me in the desire of being not-at-home too, others for respite. Still more try to find focus, even a kind of privacy, in public. Theorists describe places like this as a 'third space', distinct from work and home, and yet also part of the scene of life. Unlike the shared space of the library, where you can settle down for the day, where you are even encouraged to do so, you have to purchase a place in the coffee shop, and indeed part of the contract of being in a cafe is that this exchange of money allows some relief from the outside world – if only fleetingly. Both libraries and cafes can invite the same people over and again, as they get into a routine and create rituals for themselves, but cafes can feel more temporary, with a choreography of constantly changing occupants there for wildly different reasons.

Cafes as social hubs have a long history; people have always loved coming together to sit and talk over a hot drink, finding a few minutes' rest and relaxation in between other activities of their day. The first coffee house was opened in London between 1652 and 1654, modelled on the experience of one of the owners, Daniel Edwards. He had developed a taste for coffee while living in Smyrna (now İzmir in Türkiye) and had brought both the beans and coffee-drinking paraphernalia with him on his move to London, to the delight of his neighbours.[6] In many countries around the world, cafes continue to be affordable places to hang out, where coffee and snacks are cheap and where the crossover between day and night can be bridged: coffee served until, later, there's a transition from one kind of intoxicant to another.

For many writers across the decades, the cafe has provided an extraordinarily vibrant scene, from which life can be viewed, connections can be made and work can be done. The cafe scene of 1920s France has been immortalised in film and television, as well in writing from the era. This version of cafe life was one where creativity and conversation worked in harmony. Nestled in a corner at a little metal table, cigarette in one hand, espresso in the other, notebook in between, this cafe writer is not distracted by noise, but is in fact enlivened by it. Embedding oneself within city life is to be in among the hustle and bustle, always ready for a tap on the shoulder with some fortifying drink only a finger-click away. Ernest Hemingway's memoir *A Moveable Feast* was published posthumously in 1964, but gives an animated and age-defining version of Paris in the 1920s. As a young journalist, Hemingway had lived there in rooms of varying comfort with his wife, Hadley, and their young son, whom Hemingway rather charmingly refers to as Mr Bumby. And yet we rarely spend time with his family, except for comments from Hadley dotted here and there. Though this impression could be down to the editing (the book was altered by Hemingway's last wife Mary Welsh Hemingway), it seems as if much of Hemingway's time is spent alone, or in conversation with other writers. Many of these conversations with fellow literary ex-pats – including Ezra Pound and F. Scott Fitzgerald – are recounted in great detail, blurring the boundary between memoir and fiction. In this kinetic book, the writer is defined by that life in public. The days pass by, locations and years change fluidly, and yet Hemingway remains perpetually on the move.

What might seem so enticing in this version of writing is Hemingway's consistency: he is often pleased with his output, and dishes out helpful advice about when to start and when to stop writing. His depiction of his work combines a confident surety of his own voice with a certain kind of masculine freedom; moving between his preferred two or three cafes and a room he rents at the top of a hotel, he appears at his leisure, his life self-directed. A *Moveable Feast* opens by considering the practicalities of heating the work room he rents; a nearby cafe proves to be a much more sensible, and cheaper, solution. Hemingway describes the appealing scene: 'It was a pleasant café, warm and clean and friendly, and I hung up my old waterproof on the coat rack to dry and put my worn and weathered felt hat on the rack above the bench and ordered a *café au lait*.'[7] Settling in to his temporary workspace, he replicates a gesture of home, safe in the knowledge that he doesn't have to pay for anything more than what he drinks.

As the opening scene continues, Hemingway writes solidly in the cafe, his flow interrupted only when a young woman enters. He looks up from his writing, staring at her each time, and then declares, 'I've seen you, beauty, and you belong to me now, whoever you are waiting for and if I never see you again, I thought. You belong to me and all Paris belongs to me and I belong to this notebook and this pencil.'[8] Here Hemingway suggests that his dedication to his craft is impeded only by the possibility of sex, pitching one against the other. In another scene, however, he is more definitively disturbed by a nosey, too-familiar person, who refers to him as 'Hem', and makes fun of his working in a cafe; the control of the writer focused on work disappears, as he lets his irritation come to the fore. This swing of moods was noted at the time of publication: Douglas Grant, writing in a review in the *Times Literary Supplement* when the book was published in 1964, suggested Hemingway as both 'the bruiser and the poet'.[9] Hemingway's numerous temporary locations are mirrored in the many versions of himself we see him explore in the book.

What does it mean to be alone and in public at the same time? The cafe is determined by the possibility of interruption; it cannot be kept under strict rules, like the reading rooms of the British Library, nor can it ever be as familiar as home. What does it mean to situate yourself so definitively in among others who are not working? In the cafe, I hear snatches of conversation, sometimes intense and deeply felt, sometimes trivial. People indulge in their intimacies in private, talk straying into surprising realms – for many, the cafe is a site of words that have spilled over in a coffee-fuelled torrent, secrets shared on the spur of the moment. I too have wondered about things I may have said in public, where I have overshared, perhaps shocked a nosey neighbour. But I know that I've never felt the same acquisitiveness of Hemingway: the people around me don't belong to me or my work, and I would never set down the words I hear on the page in front of me; being in the cafe has allowed me a feeling of generosity to other people in allowing them the freedom to be as they are, and hoping this is what I'm offered in return.

This sense of freedom is also found in the possibility of simply being around others, *not* a community of writers or anyone invested in my work, but a temporary community of people of all kinds. The cafe I have spent the most time in, a short walk from my house, sees a constant flow of individuals moving in and out, some on laptops, some chatting, families at weekends or during the school holidays, older men with carers out for a walk. It's provided a stability I could never have previously imagined. Small and unfussy, it has four tables of differing sizes, a big window at its entrance through which sunlight streams or the grey of winter permeates. My ritual is set: say hello to whoever is serving, find a space and then order, sometimes a pastry, sometimes not. But though my movements might be the same, the cafe never is: I never know who will arrive, or how they will affect the atmosphere and that sense of chance is part of the pleasure.

In popular culture, cafe writers can sometimes be the butt of jokes about their (assumed) desire *to be seen* to be writing, perhaps on a novel or a screenplay. A *New York Times* article from the early 2000s names the best-known writer cafes in Los Angeles (Insomnia, Stir Crazy, Bourgeois Pig) and even outlines the unspoken rules of working on a script in public ('You are not supposed to ask anyone sharing your table what they are working on'[10]). But, Hollywood aside, this desire to be identified as a creative is not one I experience much, and given my tendency to be craned inelegantly over my computer and, in a mix of concentration and worry, forgetting to blink, I doubt many people are looking at me too admiringly. Yet the reality of the cafe community can provide a kind of safety for writers. Not through being away from home, as in the experience of Selma James, but by being nestled in among others. As the American writer Ntozake Shange noted in an interview, 'There I can write about things that are frightening or even about my own emotional development, which can also be very scary.'[11] Tackling her 'demons', as Shange calls them, seems far less daunting surrounded by other people than if she were alone in her house. Writer and podcaster Liam Bishop explained to me that 'In a coffee shop, I feel more like a participant of the world. At my favourite cafe in Leeds,

I take a spot by the window, and I can watch the busy thoroughfare in between working. Most of the time, wherever they have been in the world, [cafes] have been safe spaces ... conducive to working and reading.'[12] Dependable, almost predictable, Bishop finds that interplay between the world and himself productive but also reassuring, allowing him to slip into another mode.

Sometimes, when those bubbles of privacy are burst, it can lead to very welcome surprises and pleasures. On one rainy day, I got to chatting with my table neighbour, writer and actor Eva O'Connor, also a regular. She had commented on the book next to me – Doris Lessing's *The Golden Notebook* – and soon we were talking about everything, including her writing and mine. Later, she shares with me what she finds so entrancing about the cafe space: 'I think I am drawn to the casual nature of a cafe space, the illusion that you almost aren't working ... When I'm working in a cafe I feel like I'm there by choice (even when a deadline is looming) and I can easily escape.'[13] I recognise what Eva says here, with the additional advantage that the cafe allows for a quick exit; unlike the rigmarole of the British Library, where I have to go through various doorways before I can leave. Here, there are no demands made of me: I have nothing to prove, only that I can sit for a little while and work, before moving on.

For some, forgetting or at least removing oneself from the past, is the reason to travel. The American writer James Baldwin went to Paris in 1948, with little money, the $40 he had taken with him quickly disappearing in his first few days of finding his way in the city. Like Hemingway and his ilk, Baldwin joined a coterie of other American writers moving somewhere that seemed to hold so much literary promise. Yet Baldwin's journey was less motivated by an American's idealised version of the city as a bohemian paradise; as he later said in interviews, he left looking for a version of life less determined by the threat that Black Americans felt every day. Baldwin was a premier documenter of the contradictions inherent in American mythology, the imagined abilities of each American citizen to reach their unique potential and experience a distinct version of success and happiness, in contrast to the reality that Black Americans faced, in which that success was made all the more difficult and self-love made impossible. For Baldwin, this danger was a very real, and life-altering, one: he had known a young Black man who had killed himself by throwing himself off a bridge and he was concerned that if he stayed any longer in a country that seemed to have so much animosity to his very existence, that something violent would happen to him too, whether self-inflicted or otherwise.[14]

After he embarked on that initial journey, Baldwin would never really return; though he would take trips back to America, and become deeply involved in the Civil Rights Movement, he would always leave once more, back to Paris, spending time too in London (where he lived for a spell in the same square once inhabited by fellow American Mark Twain), in Türkiye, and finally settling for the last seventeen years of his life in a village in the south of France. In a piece for *Architectural Digest*, Baldwin refers to himself as a 'transatlantic commuter, carrying my typewriter everywhere, from Alabama to Sierra Leone to Finland'.[15] This is not to say that Baldwin was not deeply aware of the racism in Europe too, but there was something about being *elsewhere* and so often on the move that helped him see the peculiarities of white America's problem with its Black citizens more forcefully and more clearly. As Selma James found when removing herself from her home for a time, Baldwin was afforded these insights through leaving the place that had made him. In a film by the Turkish filmmaker and photographer Sedat Pakay, Baldwin neatly describes that feeling: 'One sees [one's country] better from a distance from another place, another country.'[16] This concern with place is evident in even the titles of some of Baldwin's novels: *Giovanni's Room, Another Country, If Beale Street Could Talk*, each work giving us the sense that a specific space determines the lives of its characters, and what it means to be rooted somewhere that curtails your freedoms.

In an essay documenting his early experiences of living in the city, 'Equal in Paris', Baldwin recounts his trips to the famous Café de Flore, 'where I consumed rather a lot of coffee and, as evening approached, rather a lot of alcohol, but did not get much writing done'.[17] Nevertheless, though Baldwin underplays it here, those trips to the Parisian cafe worked, and the city allowed him to fully become a writer; in the years leading up to his departure from the USA, he had been struggling for many years with the manuscript of what would become his first book, *Go Tell It on the Mountain*. In New York he had received two literary fellowships to help him write but no book had emerged; he finally completed a manuscript between various Parisian hotel rooms, the Café de Flore and in Leukerbad, a small village in Switzerland, where Baldwin was taken by his lover Lucien Happersberger. The change of scene had released something in him, allowed him greater self-knowledge: 'In America, the color of my skin had stood between myself and me; in Europe, that barrier was down.'[18]

Baldwin's literary beginnings may have started in Paris, but for Walter Benjamin, Paris was the space that allowed him to articulate many of the contradictions he saw in the twentieth century. Benjamin was German, born in Berlin in 1892, but his legacy is forever intertwined with the city through his figure of the *flâneur*. Benjamin's *flâneur*, a character borrowed from the poetry of Charles

Baudelaire, understands time and place through walking its streets, observing, glimpsing details of its past and its present living side by side. He noted how the transformations of Georges-Eugène Haussmann, the government official who oversaw Louis-Napoléon Bonaparte's complete reimagining of the architecture and geography of Paris, fundamentally altered the way that people moved through it. In the new wide streets and long straight roads, the *flâneur*, the figure of freedom, could meander, stroll and peruse the city at his leisure.

It is hardly surprising then that Benjamin was also a fan of the cafe, a space so characterised by movement, by watching and by chance. In his essay about the Berlin of his childhood, Benjamin describes how much of his social life was formed through hanging out in cafes, the essay reaching a crescendo in this very location where he is suddenly able to give shape to an idea through a drawing: 'I think of an afternoon in Paris to which I owe insights into my life that came in a flash, with a force of an illumination.'[19] Sitting in the famous Café des Deux Magots, the scene of so much literary history and just the opposite side of the street from Baldwin's spot in the Café de Flore, 'Suddenly, and with compelling force, I was struck by the idea of drawing a diagram of my life, and knew at the same moment exactly how it was to be done. With a very simple question I interrogated my past life, and the answers were inscribed, as if of their own accord, on a sheet of paper that I had with me.'[20] When he later loses the paper, he is devastated. Yet this drawing, which was to help him understand his whole existence and everyone in it, is also reflective of the sudden insights to be found because of the temporary nature of our surroundings, not in spite of them.

Benjamin's moment of clarity comes from being temporarily separated from all those important people in his life. In her memoir *The Cost of Living*, novelist and essayist Deborah Levy documents the aftermath of the more permanent separation that comes after the ending of a marriage. Once she and her now ex-husband sold what was once their family home, Levy and her daughters move to a flat in a crumbling building under a constant state of renovation. While going over the fragments of her marriage, she finds that her old life doesn't fit into this new one – furniture, books, objects crowding the new dimensions of this much smaller apartment. As well as this disjuncture between these two versions of her life, past and present, Levy also needs a new place to work. She is offered a temporary place of refuge in the shape of a shed in her friend Celia's garden. In this cold and unfussy space, with only a desk and bookshelves that Levy populates with a scant few of her most important books, she finds a voice: 'I did not know it then, but I would go on to write three books in that shed, including the one you are reading now. It was there that I would begin to write in the first person, using an *I* that is close to myself and yet is not myself.'[21] With Celia as her guard against visitors and distraction, Levy feels appreciated and taken care of, not just as a person but as a writer and a professional. After a day's work, she travels back home again, walking a long and cold route past a graveyard to make her way to her daughters. Though the route is dark and atmospheric, Levy says, 'I did not feel safe or unsafe, but somewhere in between, liminal, passing from one life to another.'[22] Later, she purchases an electric bicycle and finds her mood lifted, as if she were on holiday, not just from London but from the entirety of her previous life. Like Baldwin, who found some new shades of himself by being temporarily in-place, there comes something new from Levy's *dis*placement from the familiar: by journeying outside her marital home, she finds a revitalised sense of herself, older and more established, and able to envisage a new future elsewhere.

Levy's travel outside her home is replicated by other writers who venture much further afield in order to find inspiration. As we saw previously, Agatha Christie was never fixed on a specific writing space, though journalists always asked for her to fashion one. This might be partly because her life was so enmeshed with travel; she accompanied both her first and second husbands on respective work trips, as well as embarking on solo travelling too, including on the Orient Express in 1928, which would go on to feature in the title of her best-known, and much adapted, novel. The settings of many of her works are contrasted with the sense of Englishness often attributed to them, characterised in the divergences in her two best-known characters, Hercule Poirot, the sophisticated and neat Belgian who travels the world ably solving murders, and the diligent Miss Marple, firmly rooted in the mundanities of English village life but no less able to crack various crimes. In Christie's legacy too, we also see this contrast: she is closely associated with South Devon, dubbed 'Agatha Christie Country' by way of the walks, events and festivals that occur there, especially in and around her preserved holiday home of Greenway on the River Dart near Galmpton. But she also leaves a trace around the world, through the hotel rooms that have been created in her name, some decked out with writing spaces of their own. The Pera Palace Hotel in Istanbul, Türkiye, with a distinguished roster of guests that has included Alfred Hitchcock and Greta Garbo, proudly advertises its Agatha Christie Room. Pictures of Christie adorn the wall, and a small black Underwood typewriter (a replica of one Christie herself used, so the website copy says) sits expectantly on a side table. The copy also suggests that the author wrote *Murder on the Orient Express* here, though this isn't supported by Christie's biography. I wonder what an interested visitor would do here: are they to write, or to admire its history? The hotel has made an exhibit, something permanent, out of something temporary – the very reason one stays at a hotel, to be somewhere else, specifically *not* at home, packaged and sold to Christie's fans.

Maybe for some writers, putting their mark down on their chosen writing spot, 'imprinting themselves' as Woolf puts it, is not the most important activity and could be, in fact, a distraction from work itself. How much time could I have saved if I wasn't worrying about the look and feel of where I was writing? Maya Angelou, one of America's most revered poets and thinkers, has noted in several interviews that 'I have kept a hotel room in every town I've ever lived in'.[23] This fascinates me, the idea that Angelou's writing space is something definitively outside her home but close by, as if she can momentarily become a stranger in her own life. Angelou describes how her writing is consistent and scheduled: she leaves the house at the same time each day for the months she keeps the room. Importantly, the space becomes almost like a place out of time: 'I never allow the hotel people to change the bed, because I never sleep there . . . I insist that all things are taken off the walls. I don't want anything in there. I go into the room and I feel as if all my beliefs are suspended. Nothing holds me to anything.'[24] In her remarkable sketch, Angelou turns the writing room on its head: no longer a way of expressing the creative mind of the writer, her hotel room is deliberately bare, with all decoration removed, no possible personality evidenced, the few scant objects brought with her – 'a dictionary, a Bible, a deck of cards and a bottle of sherry'[25] – utilitarian. In this blank space she is 'suspended', forced to think only of her work. Yet, more than that, it seems Angelou looks to unhitch her very sense of self from her attachments to preconceived ideas, so that she, like the room, can become a blank canvas. Where Virginia Woolf thinks of a spider web that fastens us to the material things that make up our life, Angelou looks to discover ways to momentarily forget, even sever, those gossamer connections in order to find new freedom.

On another autumn day, I return to the Charles Dickens Museum, not to revisit the study room, but to see an item that resides in the museum's archives: his travel desk. This desk, thought to have been used from the late 1850s until his death in 1870, is made of rosewood and beautifully inlaid. As the curator Emma Harper opened the box that contained the desk, and then carefully revealed its compartments and drawers, I was filled with an uncomplicated excitement, marvelling at the objects that would have been part of Dickens's everyday life. Alongside the desk were his pen and his inkwell, which still contained remnants of ink, now dried and thin. The curator pointed out the decoration of the lid, a lion, which Dickens also used as a bookplate design. I felt the thrill of proximity, just as I had when poring over Joan Didion's catalogue.

I had hoped to hear that Dickens did a lot of novel writing on this travel desk, perhaps throughout his speaking tours that saw him travel the world. Yet my research suggested, and the curator concurred, that Dickens used the desk exclusively for his letter writing. That hadn't stopped the museum, in its very early days in the 1920s, using the travel desk to illustrate his writing scene, before they later purchased the large and imposing desk, the one that had been used in his final home of Gad's Hill Place, that stands in his study today. The real portability in Dickens's writing room was, perhaps surprisingly, embedded in some of the furniture itself: the curator explained that on the legs of Dickens's chair, as well as his desk itself, were wheels, allowing him to move furniture where he wished, as he moved between his different houses. I love that Dickens was brazen enough to do this, assert that his whole room had to come with him, that somehow the atmosphere that was made through the organisation of objects had to be transported with him from place to place.

Though Dickens may have been able to command this, most likely causing commotion for his household in the process, many other writers have found new freedoms in changes to writing tools. As academic Laura R. Micciche describes, 'Although writing's mobility might seem a product of modern digital gadgetry, there's nothing new about writing on the move.'[26] The travel or portable desk, normally made of wood with compartments for letters and writing equipment like Dickens's own, and of a size to be carried between two hands, first became popular in the seventeenth and eighteenth centuries. The famously prolific American politician Alexander Hamilton (and the subject of Lin-Manuel Miranda's wildly successful Broadway musical) composed an astonishing amount in his lifetime, including many political pamphlets and essays, and was accompanied by a sturdy desk as he travelled between states. But these portable desks didn't have to travel far to be of use, and could sometimes transform spaces of the home too, so that every nook and cranny had the potential to allow for a few moments' work. The little desk used by Jane Austen was given to her in 1794 when she was a young woman, but was a favourite object throughout her life. Her great-great-great-great niece Freydis Jane Welland describes it as 'nicely fitted with a long drawer, a place for an inkwell, penknife, and quills, and a compartment that can be opened easily with space for correspondence, spectacles and string, manuscripts and sealing wax'.[27] Austen's nephew James Edward Austen-Leigh wrote of his admiration for his aunt's output given that 'she had no separate study to retire to, and most of the work must have been done in the general sitting-room, subject to all kinds of casual interruptions'.[28] The desk provided a way for her to work without disturbing the layout of the house, or even asserting herself overtly as a 'writer'. Like Austen, all three Brontë sisters also used these desks, objects crucially both compact and practical, able to be moved out of the way and stored elsewhere when their owners were called upon to do household duties. In both the Austen cottage and the Brontë family home, these desks illustrated the need of writing to 'travel', but only as far as a few feet and out of sight of the other residents of the house. Work could be physically paused, tidied away, even if the messy business of words continued to echo in the heads of the writers long after.

When typewriters became crucial to the writing process, writing 'travelled' with it. Critic Martyn Lyons refers to the 'typewriter century' – the 100 years between the 1880s and the 1980s[29] – when the typewriter was king, before its gradual replacement by word processors and computers. Over the course of that time, the typewriter transformed the possibilities of writing, simplifying and streamlining it: no longer needing a pen and ink, the typist could imagine that they could let the words flow from inside to outside unimpeded, the idealised version of creativity. This might have partially emerged from the very basic function of the typewriter itself, an object Lyons describes as 'made *only* for writing'.[30] This exclusivity facilitates the desire of the user, it doesn't contain its own distractions – the internet, social media, email, breaking news updates, as it would be today – but instead promises so much, an object that is all potential. A cursory glance at twentieth-century adverts for typewriters show machines imbued with all sorts of enticing ideas: the American company Underwood, famed for their number 5 model released in 1899, used the phrase 'Give Wings to Words' in much of their promotional materials, often including illustrations of typewriters bedecked with actual wings. The Italian typewriter company Olivetti was renowned for their sleek designs and innovative marketing, making the typewriter not just a practical object, but a desirable one too. In many of their adverts they also emphasised the new possibilities of the machine: the 1969 adverts for their Valentine model, designed by graphic designer Adrianus van der Elst, depict the pillar-box red typewriter in a range of places, at strange angles, unattached, seemingly freed from any scene of writing at all.

For pretentious teenagers such as myself, the typewriter always seemed to be the most authentic machine for writing on (though I did dabble with a quill and ink a few times just to see if I could do it), far more romantic than my boring black laptop used for schoolwork. There was something about the typewriter in its neatness that seemed to me to *become* the entirety of the scene of writing. This scene of ceaseless production is perfectly encapsulated in the oft-repeated story of Jack Kerouac's first draft of *On the Road*, one in which the writer is so overtaken with his subject he spends three weeks in a frenzy, continuously typing on a 'scroll' – actually, drawing paper Sellotaped together – to produce over 100 feet of words. The journeying across America undertaken by the main characters, Dean Moriarty and Sal Paradise, finds an echo in the scroll, which becomes a kind of road in and of itself. The novel has been both valourised and mocked – American writer Truman Capote supposedly quipped that Kerouac didn't write the book but 'merely typ[ed] it'.[31] But the origin story of Kerouac's classic novel of the 1950s (now critiqued for its crude racism and sexism) appealed to me when I first read it at seventeen: I never bothered learning the famous brand names of typewriters Kerouac used, but in my envisioning, he became at one with his machine, transcending the 'problem' of the body and ending up in realms of pure creativity.

The typewriter changed not just the tactility of writing but even altering the soundscape we associate with it, the clickety-clack of keys becoming an underscoring rhythm to work. If no sound emitted from the room of writing, it meant that no work was being done: for Dixon Steele and Charlie Kaufman, their lack of inspiration is evidenced by the silence of their machines, the blankness of their inserted pages. On the other hand, diligent typing means productivity: in the opening sequence to the murder mystery programme *Murder She Wrote*, a favourite of mine, we watch the hands of Angela Lansbury in the role of prolific novelist Jessica Fletcher typing energetically, intercut with short clips of the adventures that fuel (or sometimes distract from) her novels. The close focus on her and her typewriter, the camera over her shoulder on the page, makes the surrounding room, seemingly her kitchen, rather incidental. She literally writes the programme into being, the words on the page in the typewriter's roller becoming the title, 'Murder She Wrote', the bouncy piano soundtrack an echo of the work of her hands.

Considering the typewriter as a transformative object might be strange now, relegated as it is (for the most part) to the past. For a while in the 2010s, the typewriter became associated with the 'hipster', a much-maligned individual found wandering in places such as Williamsburg in Brooklyn, New York, and Shoreditch in London, twirling their moustaches and drinking cocktails from jam jars. The 'hipster' was characterised by their interest in 'old' things, including fixed-gear bicycles and typewriters, essentially objects that were at their height of significance during the twentieth century. I always felt quite sorry for the hipster, and not only because I was sometimes called one by my university housemates: the hipster was mocked because they identified with things that were deemed as obsolete by modern society, looking back when they were supposed to be looking forward. By wearing vintage clothes, using a rotary phone or indeed owning a typewriter, the hipster found value in the out of date, even if it might have been a tad performative – rumours persist of writers taking typewriters to coffee shops. Not all appreciators of the past are as easily dismissed though: Hollywood actor Tom Hanks is a collector of typewriters, owning over 250. Indeed, his first book of fiction takes its title from his passion – *Uncommon Type* – its cover featuring a typewriter with a sheet of paper inserted into the roller, and a pair of horn-rimmed glasses, seemingly casually strewn across a desk. Hanks's cover hints at an unseen writer's room, firmly rooted in the look and authority of the mid-twentieth century and suggesting his own placement within that tradition of Great American Novelists. There is, in both the hipster and Tom Hanks, something undeniably precious here, evoking the need to present oneself as an authentic, somehow 'pure', creative. Hanks seems to have invented himself as a writer by associating with the materials of writing, with the romance of the 'authentic' imbued in the object of the typewriter itself. I doubt audiences would be quite as charmed if he had collected 250 different kinds of laptops.

Jessica Fletcher kept up with the times: in later series of the show, the opening title was written on a boxy desktop computer. Clearly the programme makers knew that it wouldn't make sense for her to stay committed to an outdated form of tech, given how many books she produced. The scene of writing is subject to the changes outside the writer's control, and sometimes it is the writing itself that feels temporary. Where the typewriter allowed for the production of physical copies and, therefore, multiple drafts, paper towers of discarded words, the word processor enables a writer to save their document over and over again; often, earlier versions no longer exist, records of embryonic ideas and even full sentences vanishing. As I create this book, I lose a cache of notes on a document that I accidentally overwrite when I'm not concentrating, and though there are ways of getting them back (I've watched quite a few YouTube videos on the subject), I don't persevere. Where ideas live, and how they come to fruition, has drastically changed, the technologies we use on a daily basis becoming crucial to composition in new ways, reconfiguring part of our writerly DNA. This has certainly been true for me: I used to write things out in longhand, but now everything lives on my ancient (i.e. seven-year-old) MacBook. Having both my phone and my laptop near my body, even if I'm doing something else, can feel oddly very comforting, giving me the sense that my ability to write – all of my writing tools, and all the knowledge I need to complete it – are only seconds away. As Brian Dillon has it, 'We carry our working lives in our bags or pockets.'[32] At the same time, this portability and lightness of technology makes me feel as though I could (and should) be working all the time. It can be hard to know where to identify the line, and how to switch off.

Lauren Elkin used both the constraints and potential of movement and technology to produce a compendium of the everyday in her book *No. 91/92: notes on a Parisian commute*. Written on the numbers 91 and 92 bus on her way to her teaching job in Paris, and typed into her Notes app, the book moves between the mundane and extraordinary as she charts her observations of her journeys. Unlike our other Parisian authors, Elkin's city is modern, and her writing life is reflective of that; unlike Baldwin or Benjamin she is not hanging around in cafes, her version of the city is one of commutes and early starts. In using her phone as the tool with which to compose, she looks 'to observe the world through the screen of my phone, rather than use my phone to distract myself from the world'.[33] In collecting her days, she produces a unique diary that isn't written after the fact but in the middle of things. In her comments about other people's clothes or behaviour, or later after an ectopic pregnancy and the pain of suddenly being so aware of pregnant women, her words can feel spiky and impatient; but this writing in the moment does not edit itself – Elkin even notes that she preserves some of her 'errors and omissions'[34] where they don't impede meaning.

I like that Elkin chose to forefront the shifting landscape of writing and her composition tool of choice because there is nothing precious about it; her work comes out of that day, or that evening, emerging from muddy feelings that come from close proximity with other people. This writing could happen only in those on-the-move, in-between spaces, where she wasn't at home but wasn't at work either. Noreen Masud, author of the memoir *A Flat Place*, has described how her writing is facilitated in this way too, commenting in an interview that 'I WhatsApp a lot of ideas or sentences to myself when I'm standing in queues, and load them into documents later.'[35] As with so many writers in this book, Elkin and Masud give a very real and unromanticised insight into the conflicts of contemporary life, where writing has to happen in among mundane acts such as taking public transport or waiting at the post office.

As Audre Lorde noted about poetry, novelist Keiran Goddard wonders if increasingly short and fragmented books speak directly to the conditions that produced them. When most writers work full time and submit to editors who are also underpaid, perhaps the texts we read will be 'more inclined to reproduce rather than transform the immediate context of their production'.[36] Could we map the fall in wages, the low average pay of writers and just-passing-through writing locations on the size, shape and genre of tomorrow's publications? Another author, Amber Medland, muses on how the way she writes might already have been affected by this transience: 'I'd wondered before whether writing in bars and on trains affected my style, whether all these liminal spaces made my writing ephemeral, flimsy and wholly without plot. I'd blamed the lack of space that felt like *mine* for the journals full of fragments which didn't cohere.'[37] But really, making things cohere at all seems rather amazing, when we consider how many different places our work move can be in and move through, Google Docs, emails, countless drafts, a mix of old and new technologies, hard and digital copies; and in among these varying modes of engagement are all those places of writing, at home, in the office, during an online chat; not one scene but several, and all impermanent in their own way.

What does this creation on the fly, across multiple platforms and spaces mean for preserving the writer's room of the twenty-first century? French theorist Jacques Derrida predicted this impulse to treat technology with the same reverence as other material objects in the early 2000s: 'Even the computer belonging to the "great writer" or "great thinker" will be fetishized,' he wrote.[38] A prediction that has turned out to be true, not only of other writers but of himself: three of Derrida's Mac computers were donated to the Institut Mémoires de L'édition Contemporaine, and a project entitled 'Derrida Hexadecimal' was conceived in order to trace, among other things, his playful document composition techniques (including his tendency to save various draft Word documents with punning titles). Academics and researchers have always been interested in the drafts of writers and how changes and deletions expose the most minute of creative decisions, but in this new area of the archive it becomes possible to accompany writers not only into their writing spaces but also into what they were seeing as they wrote. The physical and material archives of Salman Rushdie, which were acquired by Emory University in 2006, includes 'loose media such as floppy disks and CD-ROMs [and] four computers: one desktop and three laptops'.[39] These so-called 'born-digital' files can be accessed on a Mac that simulates the look and feel of Rushdie's desktop in 1998. Researchers can accompany Rushdie beyond the writer's room into his actual machine at the very moments of composition, finding answers to different and more esoteric questions, including what games he was playing for procrastination, aspects of the writing process that pre-digital archival research would never have been able to answer. Yet, in among all this possible 'recording' much is lost, and some things are deliberately scrubbed out: the impression we get of the entire 'recordable' past is false; like all writing spaces, this too is only a partial version.

This kind of closeness feels very eerie to me, as if the reader is no longer simply following the words a writer chooses to print but is able to stare over their shoulder at the screen itself, even counting how many open tabs they have; I can imagine Zadie Smith would be horrified. But the relationship between our body, intimacy and technology is quite noticeably strange. Sally Rooney, for example, imagines that in the moment of composition, her body completely disappears: 'I forget that I physically exist. I'm a Word document.'[40] Rooney clearly describes the state of flow, that feeling of being completely occupied with the task at hand. But there is something else too, the way that we live so closely with technology that we feel it becomes part of us, *is* us. Like Kerouac, perhaps we can all feel, through the infinite pages we can create on Word, that our words travel on endlessly.

Even if many writers feel conflicted, maybe even resent the way they compose today, preserving this version of the writing life is reflective of how the majority of them now work – the heritage of our contemporary moment. Increasing numbers of writers sell or leave their archives to institutions that consist of this mix of physical and digital archive; in the future the legacy of most writers will be made up of laptops, tablets, and even phones. Instead of whole rooms preserved in museums, we might have screens that show various versions of the writer's computer desktop, each one giving an insight into the creation of a particular book from their oeuvre, complete with accompanying notes, research and drafts. Or we might enter virtual-reality worlds that allow us to take one step further, not only accompanying the simulated writer as they compose, but writing just like them; where Joan Didion physically typed out sentences from works by Ernest Hemingway to learn his style and train her fingers, AI guides could lead us through – or more likely replicate – the very minutest details of sentence construction, line breaks, even grammar of our favourite authors. Removed from all contexts, including the writer themselves, the act of writing starts to feel ephemeral; can words produced like this still contain meaning?

These transformations in our writing technology, those things that have allowed us to take our writing with us, have found a new, and somewhat worrying, avenue in generative artificial intelligence. AI platforms promise to make all writing easy and painless, even removing the need to do any thinking whatsoever. The year 2022 saw a boom in these AI chatbots, including ChatGPT and Gemini, which, in theory, allow anyone to make 'creative' work based on a range of prompts. Writers, translators and illustrators have responded worriedly; some (less than ethical) publishers have seen opportunity. I have been following transformations in AI closely and saw its impact almost immediately in the work of my students, some of whom quickly used it as a way to dash off coursework. Chatbots seem to present a way of writing that does away with so much time, labour and effort, making everyone (and therefore no one) into a possible writer. Nonetheless, I don't think AI will see a straightforward eradication of writing as an act; in fact I suspect that some reading audiences will go the other way, demanding confirmation that what they read is in fact genuine. I know that I don't want to read a piece of confessional writing, for example, without some reality lying behind it. Like Woolf in her piece about the Brontës, concerned readers will look for what is verifiable, for some kind of legitimacy from the writers they reach for. Perhaps, even now, you too want assurance that I wrote this, that I was here, that I suffered to put these words on the page (writing on very poor sleep, or after teaching all day). In among all this potential uncertainty, the personhood of the writer might become *more* important, as publishing imprints choose in which direction to focus, marketing genre writing, fact-based titles or translations created by AI or supporting the human creators of increasingly siloed 'literary fiction' and experiential or expert-led non-fiction, among so much else that forms part of a thriving literary eco-system. How much then will the writer's room, the writer's life even, play an increasingly visible part in the way that stories are told to us and sold to us? Sally Rooney is able to keep prying journalists out, but new writers may need to prove their human credentials.

In those 'human credentials' lies something important, the need for writers to have *lives*, not to shut themselves off from all that surrounds them. The American writer Ling Ma has considered this in her own practice, as well as the advice she gives to her writing students: 'The stereotype, of course, is of the writer who just comes up with brilliant ideas in a vacuum, enclosed in a room. But you need experiences to draw on. You need to be in the world to observe it, and to observe yourself, who you are.'[41] The temporary places we find ourselves in, whether in cafes or in queues, using phones or laptops, these are all about finding that sense of the world and our connection to it. Where we might previously associate the writer with those tucked-away spaces, free to create how they wish, what so many writers have shown here is that *not* being in place can afford just as much freedom.

'Chez Baldwin' before its destruction: Saint-Paul-de-Vence, France, 2016.

Chapter 5

CHANGEABLE ROOMS

The house sits surrounded by green. The light shines brightly, seeming to make the stone of the building glow. In the garden are leafy palms, olive trees, small shrubs. A round table is shaded by a large white umbrella, the chairs around it in elegant wicker. Inside, the house is kept cool by tiled floors. A sheaf of wheat sits inside a ceramic jug perched on top of the fireplace. There are plenty of places to relax and talk.

The images fade. Parts of the house are boarded up, graffiti snaking its way up the facade. Walls crumble. For some time the room in which the writer once wrote has been exposed, its wooden shutters hanging off hinges, sunlight and rain both pouring in.

No longer private and secluded, the space is now subject to the changing conditions of the outside world.

James Baldwin's life might have been marked by travel, and by the way he could make himself at home while on the move. For the last few years of his life, however, he settled in the south of France in Saint-Paul-de-Vence, welcoming guests to sit at his inviting garden table, or taking himself off to write. The house, 'Chez Baldwin' as it became known, was so much a scene of hospitality that his final work, the unpublished play *The Welcome Table*, written in the last year of his life, is also set in a house in Provence, where a coterie of actors, photographers, journalists are hosted by the ageing diva Edith Hemings, a stand-in for Baldwin himself. Yet this house, which had been the site of so much laughter and work, has now been destroyed, developers having bought the land to turn it into eighteen luxury apartments with sea views.

Many have gone to the town of Saint-Paul-de-Vence in search of the last home of James Baldwin. More and more people look for him, as his light has shone more brightly in contemporary culture and readers mark the centenary of his birth, with groups going on unofficial tours and pilgrimages to the old location of 'Chez Baldwin'. Though his house no longer exists, it has been recorded in countless pages of essays and books in both the sombre tone of the elegy as well as quiet celebration. It's a curious feeling to write about a place that is not there and yet has such a presence in the minds of many; my account is overlaid by all those others from fans, writers and scholars alike.

When Baldwin moved into the property in 1970, he shared the building with the owner Jeanne Faure, gradually occupying an increasing number of rooms as he felt the benefits on his health and writing of his new accommodation. He and Mlle Faure had come to a strange arrangement, in which he would become the owner of the house bit by bit – an understanding that the British writer and friend of Baldwin, Caryl Phillips, explains was confirmed only 'on handwritten notes, and by word of mouth'.[1] The complex and unofficial nature of their situation would come to have a dramatic impact when Baldwin died in 1987. Baldwin's brother David moved in until 1996, with the family subsequently involved in long court cases about its ownership. In the meantime, the house sat unoccupied, losing its colours to time. The building was erased slowly, almost painfully, over several years, the demolition work stopping and starting and destroying parts of the house in isolation. As Rachel Kaadzi Ghansah wrote, 'James Baldwin lived in his house for more than 25 years, and all that was left were half a dozen pink teacups and turquoise saucers buried by the house's rear wall, a chipped fresco on a crumbling wall, and orange trees that were heavy with fruit bitter and sharp to the taste.'[2]

Though Baldwin's house could not be protected, his legacy lives on in the organisation that was created from it, La Maison Baldwin. What started out as a campaign to save the house from destruction pivoted to honour Baldwin's memory with events, talks and support, both financial and residential, for young Black writers. But why wasn't his house, Ghansah asks, preserved like those of other great American writers? This question is echoed by countless other fans of Baldwin, each of whom relay their shock that such a luminary of American letters has no house dedicated to his name. Though we may want to blame the property developer, the story of the Baldwin House also reveals much about America's history. Unlike other writers, whose relatives are able to buy properties to ensure their continued ownership in the family, or are gifted them under more secure circumstances, Baldwin's relatives could not find the money needed to cover the shortfall. This is hardly surprising, given his humble beginnings in early twentieth-century New York, the child of a mother from Maryland and a father from Louisiana who had come to Harlem as part of the Great Migration, that movement of Black Americans, from South to North, in search of better prospects. But it also goes beyond Baldwin's family to deeper problems, extending to the very material circumstances of Black Americans today, who still live with a long-lasting disparity in income: in 2019, a study showed that 'on average, Black households had 14.5 per cent of the wealth of white households, with an absolute dollar gap of $838,220'.[3] The Baldwin House reveals the central problem of preservation, that history presented in this way is premised on access to funds that, in an unequal society, will never be accessible to a large proportion of people.

History speaks in a certain voice. As this book can attest, there really is no one way of being a writer, and writers' lives have always been varied and changeable. There is, however, something to be said about the way that, for some writers, memories and legacies of their work have been transformed by their ability to be tied to specific places. This attachment can sometimes be stretched to its limits: at the very end of 2024, the residents of Alton, a town in Hampshire, created a petition to stop developers building in the surrounding green space on the pretext that Jane Austen used to visit from her nearby village of Chawton, as well as the high street being the place of work for her brother. The William Morris Gallery in Walthamstow is a wonderful space I've visited many times, but Morris spent only a few scant years in the building as a child, before his creative life began. Preservation can sometimes feel a little tenuous, saying more about what it is we want now, rather than the actual significance of what happened then. It gives an unarguable solidity to the narrative of greatness.

How does that solidity, that displayed history, alter and change the reputation of other writers? The very existence of preserved houses replicates the idea that one must have property to be a writer. It's wonderful to visit these houses, to spend time seeing if it's possible to soak up the aura of those who lived there, but not to the detriment of all those others who have left very little trace of themselves in the present through circumstance. Some writers don't or can't leave a material legacy; some houses have been altered, some destroyed, some redeveloped; some places allowed to rot and decay. The stories of these houses are often, as we see in the Baldwin House, of uninterested property developers, gentrification, or neglectful local councils. Not all writers are recognised as significant during their lifetimes or after they die, and so their houses follow suit, falling off the map. And so it is that we find ourselves, in this final chapter, stepping into the story of these changeable writing spaces with unstable pasts and futures in flux. These are rooms that existed somewhere, maybe only for a short time; rooms that may have been lived in, curated, loved, but, for whatever reason, no longer survive, either as a space or perhaps even in memory; these are rooms that may never have had the chance to exist, only ever dreams and ambitions, out of reach.

Writer, poet and activist Georgia Douglas Johnson thought about the problem of space in 1927 – two years before Woolf published *A Room of One's Own*. Writing in *Opportunity* magazine, an influential publication that aimed to foster Black literary culture and which was affiliated with writers of the Harlem Renaissance, Johnson wrote that what she needed was 'clearing space, elbow room in which to think and write and live beyond the reach of the Wolf's fingers'.[4] Johnson does not talk of private property or £500 a year but a modest boundary, physically and psychically, between herself and others. Elbow room. As Thadious M. Davis points out, Johnson illustrates not only 'the need for the economic resources to do the work of an artist' but also 'the narrow spaces of confinement in which black women artists worked'.[5]

In August 1973, Alice Walker decided to go in search of Zora Neale Hurston in her home town of Eatonville, just outside Orlando in Florida. Hurston, now a very celebrated writer and novelist, known for her work *Their Eyes Were Watching God*, died in 1960 with little money and no longer in contact with her family. Walker makes her way around the town and finds evidence of Hurston, not physically, but in people's memories: a woman who went to high school with her; a doctor who would buy her groceries when she was too frail; a neighbour who recalls her favourite flowers. Walker collects these accounts in the essay itself, and then tries to give them form in the headstone she erects at the site of Hurston's grave, which reads:

THE WRITER'S ROOM

ZORE NEALE HURSTON
"A Genius of the South"
1901 — — — 1960
Novelist   Folklorist
Anthropologist[6]

Her words pay tribute to Hurston's versatility, a keen chronicler of Southern folklore, but also a writer of complex Black characters and narratives, as well as political sensibility; she was not one thing, but several, and her intellect, in Walker's mind, needs further emphasis. For Walker, who was teaching a course on Black writers at that time, looking for Hurston in this way, and verifying her life through the solidity of a gravestone, was in direct response to the gaps she saw around her; just as Woolf looks for the history of women's writing in Britain, so Walker looks for a lineage in the US, one that she finds is sorely lacking within popular culture as well as in institutions. The way that Hurston's work had fallen out of print is repeated in the career of other Black writers, telling another story about the erasure of Black creativity from the version of American literature sold at home and abroad. Her 'preservation' of Hurston is not in the form of material but intellectual legacy, claiming another kind of space in imaginations and on syllabuses, when there are no physical spaces to point to. When we are not left with a weight of material, we have to look for them in other ways, as Walker did, seeking out unofficial, unarranged versions of writers' lives, subterranean histories that don't come with museums and plaques and walking tours.

⌒

There is still a place today for certain kinds of writing-room presentation and curation, but it must come, I think, with more thought for its function and purpose – not simply repeating paradigms of greatness. In the US, the National Trust for Historic Preservation launched its African American Cultural Heritage Action Fund in 2017, funding that has allowed for the establishing of places such as the Clifton House in Baltimore, Maryland, which celebrates the work of sculptor and philosopher Fred Clifton and poet Lucille Clifton. The two wed in 1958, and in 1968 moved to Baltimore, where Lucille Clifton was poet-in-residence at Coppin State College, and later poet laureate of the state of Maryland. The house does not boast unusual features or historic furniture: it is a family home, where the couple raised their six children, and where Lucille wrote several poetry collections at the dining-room table. The house was lost to foreclosure in 1989 but was bought back by daughter Sidney Clifton in 2019 to transform into a community space, one that would function as a corrective to the narratives of preserved and untouchable history. This house not only runs events and talks, but offers spaces for writers of colour to work through residencies each year.

In Vancouver, Canada, the Historic Joy Kogawa House, a similarly understated home on a residential street, also offers respite for both emerging and established writers. The house had been home to Canadian writer Joy Kogawa and her family from 1937, until her family was forcibly expelled in 1942, owing to the internment of all Japanese citizens after the Pearl Harbor attack. She and her family were sent to Slocan camp, many hours away inland, with all their belongings sold. Kogawa went on to write of her experiences, giving voice to the horror and trauma a generation of Japanese-Canadian citizens lived through. In recognition of the importance of Kogawa's contribution to Canadian letters, in 2006 the house was purchased after a community fundraising campaign.* It functions today as a museum, recounting a terrifying part of Canada's national history, as well as providing a personal account of Kogawa's own experience.

---

* There is some controversy about this house, as Joy Kogawa was later to discover her father, who had been a minister, was a paedophile. The trust has tried to be open about this, but some people have been upset about the preservation of the house, given this history. I think it's important to include it as the site specifically recognises the life of those in internment.

Not long after it opened, writers started to take up residencies there too. A small but striking detail can be found in the crucial object of the desk: here, it lies not behind glass like at Monk's House, or roped off as at the Dickens Museum, but available for the writers-in-residence to use. Scribbled on its surface is a missive from Kogawa herself, wishing each user well.

While Kogawa's suburban family home tells of a darker story about historic internment, filmmaker and activist Derek Jarman's Prospect Cottage seems always to have been a site of refuge and escape. A simple fisherman's dwelling of four rooms, it stands starkly black against the horizon on a shingle beach in Dungeness, Kent, an otherworldly post-industrial landscape, the nuclear power station looming nearby. Jarman wrote, filmed and gardened here, planting a wide variety of flowers and building tall expansive sculptures out of natural beachcombed materials, eking out the possibilities for growth from this landscape that looked like it would only defy it. Prospect Cottage is now a much-written-about site of queer resistance; Jarman's move to Dungeness, and the creation of the garden, came after his diagnosis of HIV in 1987, which was to be the cause of his death seven years later. His creativity emerged during a backdrop of institutional inertia against the AIDS crisis, and in the face of the homophobia most profoundly evidenced in the Section 28 law passed in 1988, in which schools were banned from 'promoting' homosexuality. He wrote in his diary on 15 April 1989: 'My garden is a memorial, each circular bed and dial a true lover's knot – planted with lavender, helichrysum and santolina.'[7]

When Jarman died, the house was left to his close companion Keith Collins, who remained the caretaker of the property for the next twenty-four years, until his own death in 2018. The building was subsequently at risk, not from destruction but from purchase by an individual buyer. After a much-publicised campaign, the organisation Art Fund raised enough money to buy it outright in 2020, helping to secure it for the future, and opening its interior to public view for the first time. Where Freud's and Carlyle's houses had their layouts sketched or photographed in order to help the preservation work that was to come, photographer Gilbert McCarragher, who had known Collins after his move to Dungeness in 2008, wanted to make a different kind of catalogue, collecting the images he produced in a book published in 2024. I'm struck by how present Jarman still is in these images, through his artworks on the walls, his bookshelves, the details of the desk in his writing room, and how he must have remained so for Collins, who lived in such close proximity with his material life after he had gone.

As with other writers' houses established in recent years, the opportunity for artists and writers to take up residencies in the house was part of the plan for the purchase of the building at the outset. As the actor Tilda Swinton, close collaborator of Jarman's, writes: 'We are not seeking to set in a time warp a precious object of historical significance for posterity only: but, crucially, to resuscitate and ensure the continued vibrational existence of a living battery.'[8] Swinton contrasts the preserved with living, the static with the changing, asserting that the project of Jarman's house must be sustained with the new fizzing energy of others who can find new ways of channelling his vision. Like the garden, with its landscape shifting through sea wind and rain, and its colours altering over the seasons, so too will Prospect Cottage experience its changing residents.

Each of these buildings continues to exist only because of work from campaigners, powerfully asserting the need of their enduring relevance through the writers who occupied them. Writers' residences in historic and preserved buildings might seem like no new thing; writers have applied for short-term stays to allow them to work at Edith Wharton's large Massachusetts house or to stay at one of Jack Kerouac's Florida homes, and visitors can even pay to spend a few hours working in the writing room of Mark Twain's Connecticut house – though not working at his desk, as I had secretly envisioned myself. The houses I've been describing here follow a different model, however, wherein its new occupants are allowed more fully to become part of the building, not just as visitors but guests of the space, using it as a base from where they can develop and grow their ideas. This seems to me to be what more writer's houses should be doing, not only celebrating the legacy of the writer in question, the solo genius who produced work while locked away in their room, but enabling that space to be shared with others. In this, these buildings move beyond reinstating the importance of these individual writers by placing their work in active conversation with writers of the future. It's perhaps unsurprising that the buildings undertaking this kind of work – Clifton's, Kogawa's and Jarman's – are also places that celebrate the memories of writers of colour, and a queer and ill writer, historically marginalised voices. In providing crucial space for others, these buildings can form a part of much-needed intervention in who gets to be a writer at all.

As spaces for creative people continue to be squeezed by all the potential barriers we've encountered in these chapters, not only rooms for writers but studios for artists too, more cultural institutions need to open themselves up further in order to address that gap: students, freelancers and others passing the time can find a spot in the Barbican or the National Theatre in London, for example, but other buildings could follow suit, placing desks in hallways, in between galleries. Even more, I'd love to see better-funded local libraries, and I fantasise about abandoned buildings, old factories, boarded-up shops, full of writers and artists who are paying cheap rent, working alone or collaboratively, and without worry. These spaces, in my envisioning, are not fancy, there are no chaises longues or mahogany desks, but there is a solidity, an anchor: writers know that this place is *for* them. Some cities already work with developers to provide somewhat more 'affordable' studios, or small-scale co-working spaces, but these are normally focused on providing spaces for artists or craftspeople. As I come to the end of this book, one building catches my eye: a collaboration between New Writing North, the writing advocacy charity, and Northumbria University that will see Bolbec Hall in Newcastle refurbished, a building originally created as supporting offices for the nearby Literary and Philosophical Society. Envisioned as a national centre for writers, Bolbec Hall will have programmes and courses, a bookshop, the obligatory cafe, but, most importantly, space for writers and students to work. Excitedly, I read the coverage of this project, wondering what kinds of writing we could have if places like this existed across the country. Giving spaces for people to work is a practical thing, but it also acknowledges writing as a worthwhile activity, a possible profession, and facilitates its continuation.

We live in a contradictory time: while authors' earnings contract, and book deals are harder to come by, there is a flourishing of books and manuals on creative writing, courses at adult education centres or specialist places such as Arvon in the UK or Gotham in the US, creative writing degrees, MAs or MFAs. There are many routes one can go down to become a writer, whether professional or amateur, and many ways in to publishing work. And yet, none of these guides or courses can adequately address the central inequalities at the root of writing nor rectify them, even with subsidised or fee-free spaces for those who need them. The National Literacy Trust noted that in 2024, '1 in 6 adults in England have very poor literacy skills',[9] and released a disturbing report towards the end of that same year which found that children's reading for pleasure was at an all-time low.[10] This is just one of the ways that things feel quite desperate for the world of words: the AI boom that disregards the importance of copyright, the funding and job crisis in higher education, removals of moderators and the proliferation of false information in the world of social media: they all affect how we think about the importance of writing and deep thought. In recent research undertaken by a group of American scholars and writers, they found that 'serious literature is more or less written by graduates of elite institutions'.[11] Without specifically addressing these gaps through government acknowledgement, action and, crucially, funding, this potential creativity will remain unclaimed, and we are in danger of never finding some writers, of never holding their words and ideas in our hands and minds.

⌒

It's been a few years since this project began and the desk for which I spent so long looking has moved. On one weekend, when the baby is old enough, he is delivered to my parents so that my husband and I can swap some furniture around. The space beside our bed, which for the last few months has been the spot where an ever-growing boy has been sleeping, is cleared, airing momentarily before my desk is hauled in. As I take each item off its surface in preparation for its short journey between rooms, I realise I have not used it for some time – instead of pencil marks, there are smudges of blue cyan, the dye my husband has been using for cyanotype animations for a film he's making about the River Lea, and instead of my books are toys that my baby no longer plays with. I was not able to keep the desk pristine, nor keep my life away from it; life has encroached, until it overwhelmed.

I live in a space that my parents own; I can do this work only because they bought this flat before I was born, with the help of gifts from both sets of their parents as well as a faraway aunt, but also when house prices were a fraction of what they are today. It was here that my parents started their life together, and it was here that became my first home, the place I affectionately called 'my little *casa*', mixing English with Portuguese. When my mum and dad decided to have another child, they realised they needed more space and an additional bedroom, and so they bought a house just a few minutes away, scrimping and saving for many years to pay two mortgages, while renting out this flat. I am able to write these words now because of their efforts and their sacrifices, as well as the advantages of class and inheritance, and their own luck growing up in a certain time and place. Now, I have the strange experience of living in the area where I grew up but that would otherwise be far too expensive for me to rent in, let alone buy. Whenever I meet new people, I feel proud to say that this is where I'm from, but I'm also saying it as a way to demonstrate that it is because of my connection to the place and my past that I am here, not because of the money I have made in my career. This is not to paint myself as anything other than privileged. I know how exceptionally lucky I am. I don't own my home but I have security that many other writers do not. This knowledge has spurred on this project, as I know that my ability to write is supported by the structures in place around me; and it is something that I want to be honest about. This book might well not exist if these rooms had not been offered to me, to my little family. What about those who do not have those same supporting structures and who cannot rely on others to help? This project is addressed to those people. One of them is my grandmother, who for as long as I have been alive has also been a writer. She arrived in the UK with my grandfather in 1970, escaping from the repressive political regime in Portugal with only a few belongings in a suitcase, pretending they were travelling for a holiday. My grandmother had limited schooling, leaving at age eleven to go and work in her father's shop; in spite of this, she is one of the most enthusiastic readers I know, hoovering up books and happily retelling me their stories. Her love of words never ceased, even when she was working long hours as a cleaner. But alongside her reading has always gone writing: she's written the history of many of our family members, and an account of her traumatic experience of lockdown when she was unable to leave Portugal to return home to England. Her story of sacrifice and of hard work is one repeated across the world, where people move from one country to another to find safety and security and better prospects. I feel increasingly how lucky I am: it is because of all her work that I can do mine. Tillie Olsen reminds us of how many of us have grandmothers like this, and how close we are to a very different kind of life, where writing anything might have seemed not only difficult, but nigh on impossible: 'Born a generation or two before, we might have been they.'[12]

The rooms we live in have a history that is only ever partly of our own making and oftentimes directly related to things we have no control over, our family and our past. Virginia Woolf was palpably aware of this. Like my parents, it is also an aunt who helps establish the life trajectory of the narrator of A Room of One's Own: 'Society gives me chicken and coffee, bed and lodging, in return for a certain number of pieces of paper which were left me by an aunt, for no other reason than I share her name.'[13] Woolf's narrator sees the inextricable relationship between money, the flimsy sound of 'paper' contrasting with the import it is given in society, and the very basic elements of her life. The aunt who wills the narrator the money is widely understood to represent Caroline Amelia Stephen, the Quaker sister of Woolf's father Leslie, who left Woolf £2,500 when she died in 1909. This money, along with legacies from the deaths of other family members, meant that fairly early on in her life Woolf had around £400 a year accrued from interest[14] (around £39,000 today) before she began to make significant money with her published work. Undoubtedly, both Woolf and the narrator tell us, that inheritance gives security and eases the way for anyone lucky enough to receive it.

These family connections and the financial inheritance that comes with them are other ways in which Woolf's writing is sometimes dismissed, but at the end of A Room of One's Own, Woolf steps in as herself, suggesting that we as the reader will have been critiquing the basic premise of the argument of her narrator: 'You may object that in all this I have made too much of the importance of material things.'[15] Woolf believed in the sensitivity of the writer, their ability to see and feel, but she also understood that that sensitivity had been prohibited from emerging for so many because of the circumstances of their lives: 'Intellectual freedom depends upon material things. Poetry depends on intellectual freedom.'[16] The older Woolf became, the more her analysis was sharpened, and the more those men of privilege, the professor in *A Room of One's Own* who writes about women while preventing them from speaking for themselves, or 'the men of professions' in her 1938 work *Three Guineas*, were the subject of her ire. In 1940, Woolf delivered a talk to the Workers' Association in Brighton, the main town close to Monk's House, in which she once more spelled out the connections between the ability to produce writing and financial circumstance, as well as the legacies of inheritance. No longer focusing on the room, Woolf instead zooms in on the way the writer's chair positions them socially, standing in for the writer's 'upbringing, his education. It is a fact, not a theory, that all writers from Chaucer to the present day, with so few exceptions that one hand can count them, have sat upon the same kind of chair – a raised chair.'[17] This striking image, a chair that sits high above the people the writer is supposed to be describing, illustrates again Woolf's keen sense of an inequity between those who are allowed to be creative due to their position in society, and those who can only be looked down on. Not only does Woolf's chair place this version of the writer 'above' others, but it actively directs the vision of what the writer sees, warping and altering it, and ultimately producing work that is only ever telling one kind of story. Woolf is undeniably well-connected, related as she is to so many of the Victorian great and good, but she used that legacy to draw attention to the fundamental unfairness of who is represented in the 'family' of literature. If the room of one's own stands for the possibility of writing, then the chair represents the step before that, the very beginnings of the creative journey.

Woolf's chair, as well as the writer it holds, remains starkly alone, strangely unmoored from that which surrounds them. So much of this book has been about that ability of writers to be alone because, in many ways, the very act of writing is premised on it. Yet I often come back to something that the Marxist critic Raymond Williams said: 'No writer is ever alone; and no man can trace the sources of all that he has taken into his own substance.'[18] Williams was thinking about influence, about voice, about style, about all the things that we absorb around us that give us a particular point of view in a certain place and time. But this quote began to take on a very different kind of resonance in the writing of this book, when so much of it came to be while I was pregnant, the most bodily way I have of *not* being alone. Many months later, when I do get to experience solitude, it is on the basis that someone else is caring for my son. In order for this to happen my husband and I rely on the labour of a childminder, partially paid for by a new government childcare scheme for children over nine months. We also rely on the proximity of my loving and generous parents who look after our son once a week and on other days too, when one of us has been ill or when we need a proper night's sleep. Even then, my sense of being alone has altered irrevocably; I am always worrying about how my little boy is doing, a hum of stress accompanying my day's activities, amplified in moments when I'm feeling vulnerable. Being alone now means being *away*. The genius author of the writer's room, the one who has taken up so much space in my mind, never had to apologise for being alone; in fact, the ability of his being able to be alone was never called into question.

Other writers have envisioned a solitude that is quite different from simply a room that keeps other people out. French writer Marguerite Duras writes how her purchase of her home in Neauphle-le-Château, France, in 1958 using the money she made from selling the film rights for her one of her very early novels, *The Sea Wall*, transformed her sense of creative solitude. In this house, Duras would go on to do much of her extensive catalogue of writing, but something else happened too, something that allowed her to find a sense of life in writing that would stay with her: 'the kind of solitude found in Neauphle was created by me. For me. And that only in this house am I alone. To write.'[19] But curiously, once Duras had found it, this solitude is one that she could bring with her, like a protective covering of her own words and ideas: 'I carried it with me. I've always carried my writing with me wherever I go.'[20] Duras's solitude is paradoxical, rooted but mobile, delimited but far-reaching; it seems to me that what she describes is the importance of a creative self-fashioning, how we can find ways to anchor ourselves in our lives and choices, regardless of place. In this mode, the writer's room is not only changeable but, as a specific place, almost irrelevant.

Alongside focusing on the possibilities (or impossibilities) of solitude, or the rooms writers don't have, could never have, I wonder then about looking for ways of making ourselves at home in the very act of writing if the physical space to do so feels elusive. My friend, the poet and writer Ralf Webb, feels the inherent resistance not in writing itself but the conditions that produce it, telling me, 'I don't really ever feel "at home" in writing because home seems to imply a relatively settled or sheltered state, and I always feel restless and creatively/financially/artistically precarious when pursuing writing, which is more or less always.'[21] I can't help but agree with the sentiment, feeling more acutely the sense of *difficulty* that is part of the lives of so many writers, even in my relative ease. Worry and anxiety can destroy the desire to create in all of us, regardless of what we do for a career, as can living in hard and fractious times, and no space, however beautiful, can overcome pain, loss and grief. This book is marked by the events of my life: as I write I get a full-time job, I have a difficult miscarriage, I get pregnant once more. The world, with its terrible wars and destabilised global order, feels dangerous and scary; continuing to write in the face of it all sometimes seems pointless, even unethical.

And still, I always return to writing as a place in and of itself, a place that calls to me, promising me a steadiness that I cannot find anywhere else. Poet and writer Bhanu Kapil writes about her experience living for a year in university accommodation for Churchill College in Cambridge after she becomes the Cambridge Judith E. Wilson Poetry Fellow. She considers her connection to the place, not only that she is 'living in the National Memorial to Winston Churchill',[22] but to the temporary nature of the accommodation itself. She muses at the conclusion of her piece:

> Perhaps I should write something
> On the wallpaper.
> Or the windowsill.
> No, this is rented accommodation.
> I will write my sentences with a fingertip.
> In the brisk, bright air.[23]

Kapil looks to the physicality of the space she rents, 'the wallpaper' and then 'the windowsill', but knows that any mark she makes or trace she leaves will be an unwelcome reminder of her existence in a place where she is to be only a passing visitor. Instead, she finds the air itself the most receptive space for her words. In invoking the intangible, Kapil draws attention to its inverse, the ability of the transient to become, momentarily, solid and real and alive. Maybe the act of writing can give us a sense of our connection, or even of making oneself at home, in places that don't necessarily feel hospitable. Kapil writes herself into the space that is not hers, that has been shared by those who have come before and will come after her.

Implicit in this are other people, even if we can't see them. The writer bell hooks thinks about balancing the solitude of writing with its direction of travel: 'Even though writing is a solitary act, when I sit with words that I trust will be read by someone, I know that I can never be truly alone. There is always someone who waits for words, eager to embrace them and hold them close.'[24] This beautiful sense of intimacy is how I want to envision being alone when I write, not something that excludes but that is always premised on the future of community. Though not everyone writes to be read, the possibility of another person waiting in the wings is in the very act itself. Being at home with writing means the possibility of companionship and of communion. Where I began the book with my writer, fuzzy and indistinct, alone in a room, that image has faded somewhat, replaced instead with an unknown person, a reader, sitting with and living with the ideas over which someone else has spent countless hours.

I return to my office on campus for the first time since my son was born. I take the train out of London on a beautiful late summer day, watching the scenery go by while thoughts of the end of this book zoom around my head. I don't write, but spend some time looking at children's clothes, listen to a comedy podcast, put on some make-up. As I arrive at my stop, I experience a strange feeling, suddenly struck with memories of the last journey I took here, while heavily pregnant, and all the other journeys I have made to and from the station over the years. I return to my office and see my little collection of postcards and photographs pinned up on the board above my desk, the painting *Dickens's Dream* by Robert William Buss showing a pensive Dickens in his writer's room surrounded by the characters of his novels, an image of Freud's room in his house in Hampstead, a scribe from the twelfth century huddled in concentrated work – a clear theme. I try to push distracting thoughts to one side: today this room is my writer's room. Yet I'm struck by how much emotion I feel in entering a little space of my own, even after so much time spent thinking about exactly this. I'm overwhelmed by my intent: over the next few hours I'll do nothing but write, filling the silence with some ASMR, a little bit of music by Labi Siffre, a song or two by Sabrina Carpenter. On my desk are newly purchased boxes of tea, dried fruit, chargers, a breast-pump. This room, which has been a site mostly of stolen sandwich bites between seminars, student conversations and gossip with my office mate, for the moment is mine; and the joy of this is hard to deny.

Throughout my time looking into the writer's room, I have continually come across other people who could have been included – more rickety kitchen tables, more rushed writing happening in between other commitments. There will perhaps be writers who you feel deserve a representation in all these versions of writing spaces and who are not here; but no book could ever contain all the variations and possibilities. Instead, what is sure is that the cultural shorthand so many of us still reach for when thinking about creativity needs changing. The image of that suffering writer in the throes of a creative block, an amalgam of so many figures of literature and scenes from films, is now rather tired. We should imagine instead a wild and various coterie of people and spaces, sprawling and innumerable: a young person scouring the internet, squinting at the screen of their ageing laptop, looking for the emails of literary agents; a writer hearing the sounds of their mother playing with their son from the next room, while they try to rush in another draft to their editor; someone in a cafe worrying if they should buy another cup of coffee to buy more time; someone else quickly typing the perfect ending to their novel into their phone while they wait for the bus to take them to work; the writer at a scratched and stained kitchen table, thinking of some dialogue, while their housemates cook dinner around them. Or me, writing these words now, a blanket round my shoulders and nestled under a thick winter duvet, working into the evening, coming to the end of a project that has preoccupied me for so long.

Each of these versions of the writing room has value in both the person and story that lie behind it. In fact, many writers, whether women, people of colour, or working-class, have, by their very existence, provided the proof that those rooms I and others imagine are not the only places where work can happen. Still more writers have looked to ways that being tethered, connected, interwoven in the lives of others, is not a hindrance but a benefit to creativity: we don't live alone, why must we create alone too? Olga Ravn thinks about this in *My Work*, finding that 'The notion that one must sacrifice everything for the sake of art – that only in this way can it become sublime – implies that anyone who is forced to take care of others, to perform manual labour, cannot become an artist.'[25] Ravn suggests that to fulfil the demands of the mythology of the writer's room, the very basic fact of life among other people must be rejected. Perhaps this is a useful way for some people to think, but as Ravn lays it out, it is also a way of creating a barrier by stealth, making demands that, as we have seen already, are impossible or entirely unwelcome. Of course, people can live to make art, but can a life be filled with *only* art and art-making? For most people, the answer would be an obvious no. I think instead of what Maya Angelou said: 'Writing is a part of my life; cooking is a part of my life. Making love is part of my life; walking down the street is a part of it . . . I think it's dangerous to concern oneself too damned much with "being an artist".'[26]

This book has not been one of writing advice; I do not pretend to have a recipe or a formula that will explain how to write, nor how to be productive. My bad habits, my procrastination, my messiness and my simple fear, have become much more apparent to me as the years have gone on; where once I may have worried about *why* I wasn't working or what it meant, I understand now that work comes in waves of shifting intensity. One cannot keep forcing out ideas – there is a limit to what can be produced in any single sitting, let alone a day. The moments where I need to read or need a change of scene seem less torturous now; I let them come, in much the same way I sometimes let words come. Yet there is something I will share: ignore the 'shoulds' of writing, and most importantly, ignore the myth of the writer's room. It will not disappear as an idea, or a reference, a question in an interview, or even as a perfect postcard image, but it might start to feel further and further away from people's realities. Maybe all of us, at some point or another, dream of easy access to an undisturbed room in which we are finally able to get on with a creative project we've always wanted to attempt. Almost 100 years after the publication of Woolf's book, perhaps we have no choice but to dream a little smaller, looking for borrowed spaces on diminished earnings. In spite of that, we can still stake a claim for ourselves in whatever form that may take; we all deserve a little space of our own. Woolf was also of this opinion, writing at the end of *A Room of One's Own* that 'So long as you write what you wish to write, that is all that matters; and whether it matters for ages or only for hours, nobody can say.'[27]

We might imagine that writing happens only in a given location, at a certain time, and in a certain pose, but writing, in its most instinctual and basic feeling, is happening always. It percolates inside us, weaving its way towards us in the day, snaking its way up as we read, or look, or simply live. We hope to trap it in the writer's room, but writing is not like an animal that can be caught and contained: it is more diffuse and changeable than that. We need not champion the genius, with all the baggage that entails, but the skill, craft and labour of the writer: we need to assert that writing is worthwhile enough to be valued and protected, wherever it takes place.

ACKNOWLEDGEMENTS

As this project attests, no writing happens alone. I have been so fortunate to be surrounded by a wonderful coterie of supportive, encouraging and loving people who have been crucial to my life as well as the book's existence: Peter Boxall, who told me the project 'had legs' when I first told him of my idea; Rachele Dini who helped me hone and shape it; Tom Knowles for his part in helping me execute the book; all my wonderful students; Charlotte Seymour who believed in the project from the beginning and provided much-need guidance throughout this process; Anna Power who steered me through the final months.

Sarah Rigby has brought a forensic eye to the book and kept it all on track; I'm so grateful for your insight as well as your patience. Additional thanks to Pippa Crane, Eluned Gulbekian, Amy Greaves, Katie Bond, and everyone else at Elliott & Thompson whose hard work brought it all together.

ACKNOWLEDGEMENTS

I have the great privilege of having wonderful friends with beautiful brains: British Library buddies Ellen Jones, Ghazouane Arslane and Will Rees have brought insight as well as levity; Kiron Ward has been my stalwart friend in this life of books; Eva O'Connor, a friend made through happenstance, a fellow mother and writer, has always believed in both me and the book; Laura Gill was a much-needed writing companion at the final hurdle. And a huge thank you to my darling girls, Beth Williams and Emily Lines, both of whom have been there for me in thick and thin. I love you all.

My family have never stopped championing me and helped me keep going. Thank you to the Powell family for your love and encouragement; to my sister Caroline, who provides an inspiration in her hard work and dedication; to my grandmother, who was writing long before I was born. And my parents who have supported me in ways that go beyond thanks. I could not have done this without you.

Finally my husband, who gave me the space to write even in the trickiest of moments: his help and love are interwoven on every page of this book. And to my son, who has completely transformed my life: you are the most joyous reason I have for not writing and not working.

ENDNOTES

Introduction

1. Sue Townsend, *The Secret Diary of Adrian Mole Aged 13 ¾* (London: Methuen, 1983), p. 81
2. Patrick Hamilton, *Monday Morning* (London: Abacus, 2018), p. 107
3. Linda Brodkey, 'Modernism and the Scene of Writing', *College English*, Vol. 49, No. 4 (April 1987), pp. 396–418, p. 396.
4. Ibid.
5. Don DeLillo, *Mao II* (London: Vintage, 1992), p. 132
6. Nicola J. Watson, *The Author's Effects: On Writer's House Museums* (Oxford: Oxford University Press, 2020), p. 2
7. Hermione Lee, 'A House of Air', in Kate Kennedy and Hermione Lee (eds), *Lives of Houses* (Oxford: Princeton University Press, 2020), p. 33
8. Virginia Woolf, 'The Leaning Tower', *The Moment and Other Essays* (London: Hogarth Press, 1947)
9. Lauren Elkin, personal correspondence, 16 July 2024
10. Jen Calleja, personal correspondence, 3 September 2024
11. Virginia Woolf, *A Room of One's Own* [1929] (London: Penguin, 1973), p. 27
12. Ibid.
13. Ibid., p. 43
14. Cyril Connolly, *Enemies of Promise* (London: Penguin, 1979), p. 137

1: The Preserved Writer's Room

1. Virginia Woolf (unsigned), 'Haworth, November 1904', *Guardian*, 21 December 1904
2. Ibid.
3. Leonard Woolf, *Downhill All the Way: An Autobiography of the Years 1919–1939* (London: Hogarth Press, 1967), p. 14
4. Virginia Woolf, 'Thursday 3 July 1919', *The Diary of Virginia Woolf*, Volume 1: *1915–1919*, edited by Anne Oliver Bell (London: Penguin, 1979), p. 286
5. Ibid., p. 286
6. Victoria Rosner, *Machines for Living* (Oxford: Oxford University Press, 2020), pp. 233–4
7. Jeanette Winterson, 'Virginia Woolf: Monk's House, Rodmell, E. Sussex', in Kate Marsh (ed.), *Writers and Their Houses: A Guide to the Writers' Houses of England, Scotland, Wales and Ireland* (London: Hamish Hamilton, 1993), p. 463
8. Ibid., pp. 46–56
9. Ibid., p. 466
10. Leonard Woolf, *Downhill All the Way*, p. 14
11. Alli Pritchard, Monk's House manager, personal correspondence, 19 October 2022
12. Watson, *The Author's Effects*, p. 94
13. Agatha Christie, *An Autobiography* (Harper: London, 2010), pp. 431–2
14. Ibid., pp. 431–2
15. Leonard Woolf, *Downhill All the Way*, p. 52
16. Ibid., p. 149
17. Thomas Wentworth Higginson, 'Emily Dickinson's Letters', *The Atlantic*, October 1891, https://www.theatlantic.com/magazine/archive/1891/10/emily-dickinsons-letters/306524/
18. Mary Ruefle, 'My Emily Dickinson', in *Madness, Rack, and Honey* (Wave Books: Seattle, 2012), p. 157
19. Sergei Pankejeff, 'My recollections of Sigmund Freud' in M. Gardiner (ed.), *The Wolf Man and Sigmund Freud* (New York: Basic Books, 1971), p. 139
20. H.D., *Tribute to Freud* (New York: Pantheon, 1956), p. 88
21. Edmund Engelman, 'A Memoir', in *Berggasse 19: Sigmund Freud's Home and Offices, Vienna 1938* (New York: Basic Books, 1976), p. 131

22. Elizabeth Hardwick, *Seduction and Betrayal* (London: Faber & Faber, 2019), p. 156
23. George A. Lumsden, 'How the House Came to be Purchased', in *Carlyle's House Catalogue* (London: Chiswick Press, 1986), p. 2
24. Ibid.
25. Ibid., p. 24
26. Thomas Carlyle quoted in Thea Holme, *The Carlyles at Home* (Oxford: Oxford University Press, 1979), p. 92
27. Jane Carlyle, quoted in ibid., p. 98.
28. Virginia Woolf, 'Great Men's Houses', in *The London Scene* [1931] (London: Daunt, 2013), p. 40
29. Ibid.
30. Ibid., p. 41.
31. Ibid., pp. 41–2.
32. Pritchard, personal correspondence
33. Watson, *The Author's Effects*, p. 112
34. Steven Connor, 'Pulverulence', *Cabinet*, 35 (fall 2009), https://www.cabinetmagazine.org/issues/35/connor.php

2: The Writer's Room in Public

1. Sophie Haigney, *The Paris Review*, 17 November 2022, https://www.theparisreview.org/blog/2022/11/17/at-the-joan-didion-estate-sale/
2. Ibid.
3. Rebecca Roach '"Do You Use a Pencil or a Pen?": Author Interviews as Literary Advice', in Anneleen Masschelein and Dirk de Geest (eds), *Writing Manuals for the Masses. New Directions in Book History* (London: Palgrave Macmillan, 2021), p. 345
4. Hilary Mantel, 'Can These Bones Live?', *The Reith Lectures*, 2017, Radio 4, https://www.bbc.co.uk/programmes/b08wp3g3
5. *Time* magazine, 12 April 1937, https://content.time.com/time/covers/0,16641,19370412,00.html
6. Editorial, ibid., https://time.com/archive/6778966/books-how-time-passes/
7. Ibid.

8. Roxane Gay, 'Someday Everything Will Matter: Shit Fancy Writers Say', *HTML Giant*, 15 June 2012, https://htmlgiant.com/web-hype/someday-everything-will-matter-shit-fancy-writers-say/
9. Joyce Carol Oates, @JoyceCarolOates, Twitter/X, 16 March 2021, 4.23, https://x.com/JoyceCarolOates/status/1371859718650597387?lang=en
10. Christian Lorentzen, 'Like This or Die', *Harpers*, April 2019, https://harpers.org/archive/2019/04/like-this-or-die/
11. Zadie Smith, on Charlie Rose, YouTube, uploaded by Remembrance of Things Past, 27 March 2020, https://www.youtube.com/watch?v=5IS6W1dnSec
12. Zadie Smith, in conversation with Christopher Bollen, *Interview*, 24 August 2012, https://www.interviewmagazine.com/culture/zadie-smith
13. Lauren Oyler, 'The Thou of Zadie Smith', *Baffler*, 6 February 2018, https://thebaffler.com/latest/the-thou-of-zadie-smith-oyler
14. Ibid.
15. Andrea Long Chu, 'How Zadie Smith Lost Her Teeth', *Vulture*, 5 September 2023, https://www.vulture.com/article/zadie-smith-the-fraud-review.html
16. Sally Rooney, in interview with Róisín Ingle, *Irish Times*, 4 September 2021, https://www.irishtimes.com/culture/books/sally-rooney-i-m-really-paranoid-about-my-personal-life-i-feel-self-conscious-1.4655068
17. Sally Rooney, in interview with Martin Doyle, *Irish Times*, 24 September 2024, https://www.irishtimes.com/culture/books/2024/09/14/sally-rooney-there-is-something-christian-about-my-work-even-if-i-would-not-describe-myself-as-religious/
18. Hilary Mantel, in interview with Alex Clark, *Guardian*, 22 February 2020 https://www.theguardian.com/books/2020/feb/22/hilary-mantel-ive-got-quite-amused-at-people-saying-i-have-writers-block-ive-been-like-a-factory
19. Geoff Dyer, 'The Art of Nonfiction', *The Paris Review*, Issue 207 (winter 2013), https://www.theparisreview.org/interviews/6282/the-art-of-nonfiction-no-6-geoff-dyer
20. Grace Cook, 'Rooms of their own', *Financial Times*, 22 April 2022, https://www.ft.com/content/74c530ac-304f-4905-a457-d0bb5837007f
21. Brian Dillon, *I Am Sitting in a Room* (New York: Cabinet Books, 2011), p. 60
22. Emily Cooper, personal correspondence, 27 July 2023
23. Justin Russell Greene, 'Dressing up the author: Jonathan Franzen and David Foster Wallace branding their masculine authorial identities through fashion', *Fashion, Style & Popular Culture*, Vol. 7, No. 4 (2020), pp. 421–41, p. 426

24. Constance Grady, 'The rise and fall and rise again of Jonathan Franzen', *Vox*, 9 October 2021, https://www.vox.com/culture/22691692/jonathan-franzen-controversy-crossroads-oprah-franzenfreude
25. Rosemary Hill, 'Short Cuts', *London Review of Books*, Vol. 39. No. 15 (27 July 2017), https://www.lrb.co.uk/the-paper/v39/n15/rosemary-hill/short-cuts
26. Melissa Young, 'How to Look Like a Writer', WikiHow, https://www.wikihow.com/Look-Like-a-Writer
27. Bougie London Literary Woman, @BougieLitWoman, Twitter/X, 18 November 2018, 5.53
28. Ibid., 20 November 2018, 8.59
29. Ali Smith 'The Art of Fiction no. 36', interview by Adam Begley, *The Paris Review*, 221 (summer 2017), https://www.theparisreview.org/interviews/6949/the-art-of-fiction-no-236-ali-smith
30. Raven Leilani, in interview with Jennifer Wilson, *Lux*, Issue 2, https://lux-magazine.com/article/raven-leilani-needs-to-know-how-her-characters-pay-rent/
31. Becca Rothfeld, 'Normal Novels', *The Point*, 28 January 2020, https://thepointmag.com/criticism/normal-novels/

3: Shared Spaces

1. George Orwell, *Keep the Aspidistra Flying* (London: Penguin, 1989), p. 33
2. Ibid.
3. Press release, 'At least 354,000 people homeless in England today', Shelter, 11 December 2024, https://england.shelter.org.uk/media/press_release/at_least_354000_people_homeless_in_england_today_
4. Kath Scanlon, Fanny Blanc, Annie Edge and Christine Whitehead, 'The Bank of Mum and Dad: How it *Really* Works', LSE Report for Family Building Society, January 2019, https://www.lse.ac.uk/business/consulting/assets/documents/the-bank-of-mum-and-dad.pdf, p. 1
5. Kit de Waal, 'Make room for working class writers', *Guardian*, 10 February 2018, https://www.theguardian.com/books/2018/feb/10/kit-de-waal-where-are-all-the-working-class-writers-
6. Michael Magee, in Lafarge et al., '"Our rental system is rigged": young novelists on their generation's housing crisis', 23 April 2023, https://www.

ENDNOTES

theguardian.com/books/2023/apr/23/uk-rental-market-housing-crisis-writers-authors

7. Amy Thomas, Michele Battisti and Martin Kretschmer, 'UK Authors' Earning and Contracts 2022: A Survey of 60,000 Writers', CreatE, University of Glasgow, p. 7
8. Daisy Lafarge, in Lafarge et al., '"Our rental system is rigged": young novelists on their generation's housing crisis'
9. 'History', The British Museum, https://www.britishmuseum.org/about-us/british-museum-story/history
10. Virginia Woolf, *A Room of One's Own*, p. 35
11. Ruth Hoberman, 'Women in the British Museum Reading Room during the late-nineteenth and early-twentieth centuries: from quasi-to counterpublic', *Feminist Studies*, 22 September 2002
12. Antonio Panizzi, quoted in Edward Miller, 'Antonio Panizzi and the British Museum', *The British Library Journal*, Vol. 5, No. 1 (1979), p. 6
13. Andrew Pettegree and Arthur der Weduwen, *Library: A Fragile History* (London: Profile, 2021), p. 280
14. James Baldwin, *Go Tell It on the Mountain* (London: Michael Joseph, 1974), pp. 42–3
15. Ibid. p. 43
16. Alexandra Schwartz, 'Sheila Heti wrestles with a big decision in "Motherhood"', *The New Yorker*, 20 April 2018, https://www.newyorker.com/magazine/2018/05/07/sheila-heti-wrestles-with-a-big-decision-in-motherhood
17. Charlotte Perkins Gilman, *The Yellow Wallpaper* (London: Virago, 1981), p. 12
18. Ibid. p. 13
19. Simone de Beauvoir, *The Second Sex*, trans. Constance Borde and Sheila Malovany-Chevallier (London: Jonathan Cape, 2009), p. 487
20. Rachel Cusk, *A Life's Work* (London: Faber & Faber, 2019), p. 144
21. Roland Barthes, 'Novels and Children', in *Mythologies*, trans. Annette Lavers (London: Vintage, 2009), p. 50
22. Woolf, *A Room of One's Own*, p. 27
23. Ian Watt, *Rise of the Novel* (London: Penguin, 1966), p. 310
24. Woolf, *A Room of One's Own*, p. 105
25. Alta, *Momma: A Start on all the Untold Stories* (Times Change Press, 1974), p. 13

26. Ibid. p. 34
27. Tillie Olsen, *Silences* (London: Virago, 1979), p. 39
28. J. G. Ballard, *Miracles of Life* (London: Fourth Estate, 2008), p. 226
29. Bea Ballard, 'My dad, the perfect mum', *Bea Ballard*, 26 April, 2009, https://www.beaballard.com/writing-bea-ballard/jg-ballard
30. J. G. Ballard, *Miracles of Life*, p. 227
31. Alta, *Momma*, p. 14
32. Iris Marion Young, 'House and Home: Feminist Variations on a Theme', in *On Female Body Experience: 'Throwing Like a Girl' and Other Essays* (Oxford: Oxford University, 2006), p. 138
33. Judith Kerr, in interview with Candice Pires, *Guardian*, 4 March 2017, https://www.theguardian.com/lifeandstyle/2017/mar/04/house-where-tiger-came-to-tea-judith-kerr-candice-pires
34. Ibid.
35. Ursula Le Guin, in interview with Julie Phillips, *The New Yorker*, 10 October 2016, https://www.newyorker.com/magazine/2016/10/17/the-fantastic-ursula-k-le-guin
36. Barbara Smith, 'A Press of Our Own Kitchen Table: Women of Color Press', *Frontiers: A Journal of Women's Studies*, Vol. 10, No. 3 (1989), p. 11
37. Paule Marshall, 'Poets in the Kitchen', *Callaloo*, Vol. 24, No. 2 (spring 2001), p. 628
38. Ibid, p. 629
39. Elizabeth Gaskell, *The Life of Charlotte Bronte*, Volume 1 (New York: D. Appleton, 1857), p. 39
40. Elizabeth Gaskell, *The Life of Charlotte Bronte*, Volume 2 (New York: D. Appleton, 1857), p. 9
41. Dennis Potter, *The Singing Detective*, directed by Jon Amiel, BBC, 1986
42. Carlo Kureishi, 'My father was paralysed, now I must be his voice', YouTube, uploaded by Times Radio, 17 January 2023, https://www.youtube.com/watch?v=ph11V2W9wuA&ab_channel=TimesRadio
43. Hanif Kureishi, 'If Not for You', *The Kureishi Chronicles*, Substack, 29 June 2024, https://hanifkureishi.substack.com/p/writing-and-collaboration
44. Hanif Kureishi, 'Sitting Down with You Everyday', *The Kureishi Chronicles*, Substack, 17 August 2024, https://hanifkureishi.substack.com/p/sitting-down-with-you-everyday

45. Amber Medland, in Lafarge et al., '"Our rental system is rigged": young novelists on their generation's housing crisis'
46. Buchi Emecheta, *Second Class Citizen* (London: Heinemann Educational Publishers, 1994), n.p.

4: Temporary Spaces

1. Virginia Woolf, 'Sunday 26 January', *The Diary of Virginia Woolf*, Volume 3: *1925–1930*, edited by Anne Oliver Bell and Andre McNeillie (London: Harcourt Brace Jovanovich, 1980), p. 285
2. Gloria E. Anzaldúa, 'Speaking in Tongues . . .', in *This Bridge Called My Back*, edited by Cherríe L. Moraga and Gloria E. Anzaldúa (Berkeley: Third Woman Press, 2002), p. 189
3. Tillie Olsen, *Silences*, pp. 10–11
4. Audre Lorde, 'Age, Race, Class, and Sex', in *Sister Outsider* (London: Penguin, 2019), p. 109
5. Selma James, 'Introduction to A Woman's Place', in *Sex, Race and Class* (London: PM Press, 2012), p. 12
6. Markman Ellis, *The Coffee-House: A Cultural History* (London: Phoenix, 2005), pp. 26–8
7. Ernest Hemingway, *A Moveable Feast* (London: Vintage, 2000), p. 4
8. Ibid, p. 5
9. Douglas Grant, 'The bruiser and the poet', *Times Literary Supplement*, 21 May 1964, https://www.the-tls.co.uk/regular-features/from-the-archive/the-bruiser-and-the-poet-hemingway-douglas-grant-from-the-archive
10. Janelle Brown, 'For Screenwriters, Inspiration Smells Like French Roast', *New York Times*, 16 May 2004, https://www.nytimes.com/2004/05/16/style/for-screenwriters-inspiration-smells-like-french-roast.html
11. Ntozake Shange, in interview with Claudia Tate, *Black Women Writers at Work* (Chicago: Haymarket Books, 1983).
12. Liam Bishop, personal correspondence, 30 August 2024
13. Eva O'Connor, personal correspondence, 21 September 2024
14. James Baldwin, 'The Art of Fiction no. 78', in interview with Jordan Elgrably, *The Paris Review*, Issue 91 (spring 1984), https://www.theparisreview.org/interviews/2994/the-art-of-fiction-no-78-james-baldwin

15. James Baldwin, quoted in Magdalena J. Zaborowska, *Me and My House* (London: Duke University Press, 2018), p. 53
16. James Baldwin, quoted in Magdalena J. Zaborowska, *James Baldwin's Turkish Decade* (London: Duke University Press, 2008), p. 18
17. James Baldwin, 'Equal in Paris' in *Notes of a Native Son: Collected Essays* (New York: Library of Congress, 1998) p. 100
18. James Baldwin, 'Introduction' in *Nobody Knows my Name* in *Notes of a Native Son*, p. 134
19. Walter Benjamin, 'Berlin Childhood', *One Way Street*, trans. Edmund Jephcott and Kingsley Shorter (London: Harcourt Brace Jovanovich, 1978), p. 318
20. Ibid.
21. Deborah Levy, *The Cost of Living* (London: Penguin, 2019), p. 44
22. Ibid, p. 56.
23. Maya Angelou, 'The Art of Fiction no. 119', interviewed by George Plimpton, *The Paris Review*, Issue 116 (fall 1990), https://www.theparisreview.org/interviews/2279/the-art-of-fiction-no-119-maya-angelou
24. Ibid.
25. Maya Angelou, interviewed by Claudia Tate, *Black Women Writers at Work*, p. 28
26. Laura R. Micciche, 'Writers have always loved mobile devices', *The Atlantic*, 18 August 2018, https://www.theatlantic.com/technology/archive/2018/08/writers-have-always-loved-mobile-devices/567637/
27. Freydis Jane Welland, 'The History of Jane Austen's Writing Desk', *Persuasions*, 20 (2008), p. 128
28. James Edward Austen-Leigh, *A Memoir of Jane Austen* (London: Richard Bentley, 1870), p. 102
29. Martyn Lyons, *The Typewriter Century* (Toronto: University of Toronto Press, 2021), p. 13
30. Ibid., p. 188
31. Truman Capote, quoted in ibid., p. 6
32. Dillon, *I'm Sitting in a Room*, p. 47
33. Lauren Elkin, *No. 91/92: notes on a Parisian commute* (London: Les Fugitives, 2021), p. xi
34. Ibid., p. xiii
35. Noreen Masud, 'Shelf Life', *Lunate*, 8 August 2024, https://www.lunate.co.uk/features/noreen-masuds-shelf-life

ENDNOTES

36. Keiran Goddard, '"Secure, affordable homes are the stuff of fiction": how young writers are responding to the UK housing crisis', *Guardian*, 3 February 2024, https://www.theguardian.com/books/2024/feb/03/secure-affordable-homes-are-the-stuff-of-fiction-how-young-writers-are-responding-to-the-uk-housing-crisis
37. Medland, in Lafarge et al., "'Our rental system is rigged'"
38. Jacques Derrida, *Paper Machine*, trans. Rachel Bowlby (Stanford: Stanford University Press, 2005), p. 29
39. Porter Olsen, 'Emulation as Mimicry: Reading the Salman Rushdie Digital Archive', *South Asian Review*, Vol. 40, No. 3 (2019), p. 176
40. Sally Rooney, 'Loving the Limitations of the Novel: A Conversation between Sally Rooney and Merve Emre', *The Paris Review*, 9 October 2024, https://www.theparisreview.org/blog/2024/10/09/loving-the-limitations-of-the-novel-a-conversation-between-sally-rooney-and-merve-emre/
41. Ling Ma, in conversation with Jess Focht, 'On Committing to Wasting Time', *The Creative Independent*, 2 October 2023, https://thecreativeindependent.com/people/writer-ling-ma-on-committing-to-wasting-time/

5: Changeable Rooms

1. Caryl Phillips, 'A house is not a home', *Times Literary Supplement*, 6 December 2024, https://www.the-tls.co.uk/lives/biography/the-importance-of-place-to-james-baldwin-essay-caryl-phillips
2. Rachel Kaadzi Ghansah, 'The Weight of James Arthur Baldwin', *Buzzfeed*, 29 February 2016, https://www.buzzfeed.com/rachelkaadzighansah/the-weight-of-james-arthur-baldwin-203
3. Christian E. Weller and Lily Roberts, 'Eliminating the Black-White Wealth Gap is a Generational Challenge', *American Progress*, 19 March 2021, https://www.americanprogress.org/article/eliminating-black-white-wealth-gap-generational-challenge/
4. Georgia Douglas Johnson, quoted in Thadious M. Davis, 'Black Women's Modernist Literature', *Cambridge Companion to Modernist Women Writers* (Cambridge: Cambridge University Press, 2010), p. 95
5. Ibid.
6. Alice Walker, *In Search of Our Mother's Gardens* (London: Phoenix Books, 2005), p. 107.

7. Derek Jarman, *Modern Nature* (Minneapolis: University of Minnesota Press, 2009), p. 55
8. Tilda Swinton, 'Residences', *Prospect Cottage – Creative Folkestone*, January 2020, https://www.creativefolkestone.org.uk/prospect-cottage/residencies/
9. 'Adult Literacy Rates', *National Literacy Trust*, https://literacytrust.org.uk/parents-and-families/adult-literacy
10. 'Reading for Pleasure', *National Literacy Trust*, https://literacytrust.org.uk/reading-for-pleasure/
11. Claire Grossman, Stephanie Young and Juliana Spahr, 'Who Gets to Be a Writer?', *Public Books*, 15 April 2021, https://www.publicbooks.org/who-gets-to-be-a-writer
12. Tillie Olsen, *Silences*, p. 184
13. Virginia Woolf, *A Room of One's Own*, p. 38
14. Clara Jones, 'Virginia Woolf's *A Room of One's Own* and the Problem of Inherited Wealth', in Emily J. Hogg and Clara Jones (eds), *Influence and Inheritance in Feminist English Studies* (Basingstoke: Palgrave Macmillan, 2015), p. 25
15. Woolf, *A Room of One's Own*, p. 105
16. Ibid., p. 106
17. Woolf, 'The Leaning Tower', p. 111
18. Raymond Williams, *Drama in Performance* (London: Frederick Muller, 1954), p. iv
19. Marguerite Duras, *Writing*, trans. Mark Polizzotti (Minneapolis: University of Minnesota Press, 2011), p. 1
20. Ibid., p. 2
21. Ralf Webb, personal correspondence, 27 January 2025
22. Bhanu Kapil, 'Tenancy Part 10: Notes Upon Return', *Map*, January 2021, https://mapmagazine.co.uk/tenancy-part-10-notes-upon-return
23. Ibid.
24. bell hooks, *Remembered Rapture: The Writer at Work* (London: Women's Press, 1993), p. 13
25. Olga Ravn, *My Work*, trans. Sophia Hersi Smith and Jennifer Russell (London: Lolli, 2023), p. 323
26. Maya Angelou, quoted in Tate, *Black Women Writers at Work*, p. 25
27. Woolf, *A Room of One's Own*, p. 105

BIBLIOGRAPHY

'Adult Literacy Rates', *National Literacy* Trust, https://literacytrust.org.uk/parents-and-families/adult-literacy

Alta, *Momma: A Start on all the Untold Stories* (Times Change Press, 1974)

Angelou, Maya, 'The Art of Fiction no. 119', interviewed by George Plimpton, *The Paris Review*, Issue 116 (fall 1990), https://www.theparisreview.org/interviews/2279/the-art-of-fiction-no-119-maya-angelou

Austen-Leigh, James Edward, *A Memoir of Jane Austen* (London: Richard Bentley, 1870)

Baldwin, James, *Go Tell It on the Mountain* (London: Michael Joseph, 1974)

——, 'The Art of Fiction no. 78' in interview with Jordan Elgrably, *The Paris Review*, Issue 91 (spring 1984), https://www.theparisreview.org/interviews/2994/the-art-of-fiction-no-78-james-baldwin

——, *Notes of a Native Son: Collected Essays* (New York: Library of Congress, 1998)

Ballard, Bea, 'My dad, the perfect mum', *Bea Ballard*, 26 April, 2009, https://www.beaballard.com/writing-bea-ballard/jg-ballard

Ballard, J. G., *Miracles of Life* (London: Fourth Estate, 2008)

Barthes, Roland, *Mythologies*, trans. Annette Lavers (London: Vintage, 2009)

Beauvoir, Simone de, *The Second Sex*, trans. Constance Borde and Sheila Malovany-Chevallier (London: Jonathan Cape, 2009)

Benjamin, Walter, 'Berlin Childhood', *One Way Street*, trans. Edmund Jephcott and Kingsley Shorter (London: Harcourt Brace Jovanovich, 1978)

Bishop, Liam, personal correspondence, 30 August 2024

Bougie London Literary Woman, @BougieLitWoman, Twitter/X, 18 November 2018, 5.53

——, @BougieLitWoman, Twitter/X, 20 November 2018, 8.59

BIBLIOGRAPHY

Brodkey, Linda, 'Modernism and the Scene(s) of Writing', *College English*, Vol. 49, No. 4 (April 1987), pp. 396–418

Brown, Janelle, 'For Screenwriters, Inspiration Smells Like French Roast', *The New York Times*, 16 May 2004, https://www.nytimes.com/2004/05/16/style/for-screenwriters-inspiration-smells-like-french-roast.html

Calleja, Jen, personal correspondence, 3 September 2024

Christie, Agatha, *An Autobiography* (London: Harper, 2010)

Chu, Andrea Long, 'How Zadie Smith Lost Her Teeth', *Vulture*, 5 September 2023, https://www.vulture.com/article/zadie-smith-the-fraud-review.html

Connolly, Cyril, *Enemies of Promise* (London: Penguin, 1979)

Connor, Steven, 'Pulverulence', *Cabinet*, 35 (fall 2009), https://www.cabinetmagazine.org/issues/35/connor.php

Cook, Grace, 'Rooms of their own', *Financial Times*, 22 April 2022, https://www.ft.com/content/74c530ac-304f-4905-a457-d0bb5837007f

Cooper, Emily, personal correspondence, 27 July 2023

Cusk, Rachel, *A Life's Work* (London: Faber & Faber, 2019)

Davis, Thadious M., 'Black Women's Modernist Literature', in *Cambridge Companion to Modernist Women Writers* (Cambridge: Cambridge University Press, 2010)

DeLillo, Don, *Mao II* (London: Vintage, 1992)

Derrida, Jacques, *Paper Machine*, trans. Rachel Bowlby (Stanford University Press, 2005)

Dillon, Brian, *I Am Sitting in a Room* (New York: Cabinet Books, 2011)

Duras, Marguerite, *Writing*, trans. Mark Polizzotti (Minneapolis: University of Minnesota Press, 2011)

Dyer, Geoff, 'The Art of Nonfiction', *The Paris Review*, Issue 207 (winter 2013), https://www.theparisreview.org/interviews/6282/the-art-of-nonfiction-no-6-geoff-dyer

Elkin, Lauren, *No. 91/92: notes on a Parisian commute* (London: Les Fugitives, 2021)

——, personal correspondence, 16 July 2024

Ellis, Markman, *The Coffee-House: A Cultural History* (London: Phoenix, 2005)

Emecheta, Buchi, *Second Class Citizen* (London: Heinemann Educational Publishers, 1994)

Engelman, Edmund, 'A Memoir', in *Berggasse 19: Sigmund Freud's Home and Offices, Vienna 1938* (New York: Basic Books, 1976)

Gaskell, Elizabeth, *The Life of Charlotte Bronte*: Volume 1 (New York: D. Appleton, 1857)

——, *The Life of Charlotte Bronte*: Volume 2 (New York: D. Appleton, 1857)

Gay, Roxane, 'Someday Everything Will Matter: Shit Fancy Writers Say', *HTML Giant*, 15 June 2012, https://htmlgiant.com/web-hype/someday-everything-will-matter-shit-fancy-writers-say/

Ghansah, Rachel Kaadzi, 'The Weight of James Arthur Baldwin', *Buzzfeed*, 29 February 2016, https://www.buzzfeed.com/rachelkaadzighansah/the-weight-of-james-arthur-baldwin-203

Gilman, Charlotte Perkins, *The Yellow Wallpaper* (London: Virago, 1981)

Goddard, Keiran, '"Secure, affordable homes are the stuff of fiction": how young writers are responding to the UK housing crisis', *Guardian*, 3 February 2024, https://www.theguardian.com/books/2024/feb/03/secure-affordable-homes-are-the-stuff-of-fiction-how-young-writers-are-responding-to-the-uk-housing-crisis

Grady, Constance, 'The rise and fall and rise again of Jonathan Franzen', *Vox*, 9 October 2021, https://www.vox.com/culture/22691692/jonathan-franzen-controversy-crossroads-oprah-franzenfreude

Grant, Douglas, 'The bruiser and the poet', *Times Literary Supplement*, 21 May 1964, https://www.the-tls.co.uk/regular-features/from-the-archive/the-bruiser-and-the-poet-hemingway-douglas-grant-from-the-archive

Greene, Justin Russell, 'Dressing up the author: Jonathan Franzen and David Foster Wallace branding their masculine authorial identities through fashion', *Fashion, Style & Popular Culture*, Vol. 7, No. 4 (2020), pp. 421–41

Grossman, Claire, Stephanie Young and Juliana Spahr, 'Who Gets to Be a Writer?', *Public Books*, 15 April 2021, https://www.publicbooks.org/who-gets-to-be-a-writer

H.D., *Tribute to Freud* (New York: Pantheon, 1956)

Haigney, Sophie, *The Paris Review*, 17 November 2022, https://www.theparisreview.org/blog/2022/11/17/at-the-joan-didion-estate-sale/

Hamilton, Patrick, *Monday Morning* (London: Abacus, 2018)

Hardwick, Elizabeth, *Seduction and Betrayal* (London: Faber & Faber, 2019)

BIBLIOGRAPHY

Hemingway, Ernest, *A Moveable Feast* (London: Vintage, 2000)

Higginson, Thomas Wentworth, 'Emily Dickinson's Letters', *The Atlantic*, October 1891, https://www.theatlantic.com/magazine/archive/1891/10/emily-dickinsons-letters/306524/

Hill, Rosemary, 'Short Cuts', *London Review of Books*, Vol. 39, No. 15 (27 July 2017), https://www.lrb.co.uk/the-paper/v39/n15/rosemary-hill/short-cuts

Hoberman, Ruth, 'Women in the British Museum Reading Room during the late-nineteenth and early-twentieth centuries: from quasi- to counterpublic', *Feminist Studies*, 22 September 2002

Holme, Thea, *The Carlyles at Home* (Oxford: Oxford University Press, 1979)

hooks, bell, *Remembered Rapture: The Writer at Work* (London: Women's Press, 1993)

James, Selma, 'A Woman's Place', in *Sex, Race and Class* (London: PM Press, 2012)

Jarman, Derek, *Modern Nature* (Minneapolis: University of Minnesota Press, 2009)

Jones, Clara, 'Virginia Woolf's *A Room of One's Own* and the Problem of Inherited Wealth' in Emily J. Hogg and Clara Jones (eds), *Influence and Inheritance in Feminist English Studies* (Basingstoke: Palgrave Macmillan, 2015)

Kapil, Bhanu, 'Tenancy Part 10: Notes Upon Return', *Map*, January 2021, https://mapmagazine.co.uk/tenancy-part-10-notes-upon-return

Kennedy, Kate, and Hermione Lee (eds), *Lives of Houses* (Oxford: Princeton University Press, 2020)

Kerr, Judith, in interview with Candice Pires, *Guardian*, 4 March 2017, https://www.theguardian.com/lifeandstyle/2017/mar/04/house-where-tiger-came-to-tea-judith-kerr-candice-pires

Kureishi, Carlo, 'My father was paralysed, now I must be his voice', YouTube, uploaded by Times Radio, 17 January 2023, https://www.youtube.com/watch?v=ph11V2W9wuA&ab_channel=TimesRadio

Kureishi, Hanif, 'If Not for You', *The Kureishi Chronicles*, Substack, 29 June 2024, https://hanifkureishi.substack.com/p/writing-and-collaboration

——, 'Sitting Down with You Everyday', *The Kureishi Chronicles*, Substack, 17 August 2024, https://hanifkureishi.substack.com/p/sitting-down-with-you-everyday

Lafarge, Daisy, Nzelu Okechukwu, Amber Medland and Michael Magee, '"Our rental system is rigged": young novelists on their generation's housing crisis', *Guardian*, 23 April 2023, https://www.theguardian.com/books/2023/apr/23/uk-rental-market-housing-crisis-writers-authors

BIBLIOGRAPHY

Le Guin, Ursula, in interview with Julie Phillips, *The New Yorker*, 10 October 2016, https://www.newyorker.com/magazine/2016/10/17/the-fantastic-ursula-k-le-guin

Leilani, Raven, in interview with Jennifer Wilson, *Lux*, Issue 2, https://lux-magazine.com/article/raven-leilani-needs-to-know-how-her-characters-pay-rent/

Levy, Deborah, *The Cost of Living* (London: Penguin, 2019)

Lorde, Audre, *Sister Outsider* (London: Penguin, 2019)

Lorentzen, Christian, 'Like This or Die', *Harper's*, April 2019, https://harpers.org/archive/2019/04/like-this-or-die/

Lumsden, George A., 'How the House Came to be Purchased', in *Carlyle's House Catalogue* (London: Chiswick Press, 1986)

Lyons, Martyn, *The Typewriter Century* (Toronto: University of Toronto Press, 2021)

Ma, Ling, in conversation with Jess Focht, 'On Committing to Wasting Time', *The Creative Independent*, 2 October 2023, https://thecreativeindependent.com/people/writer-ling-ma-on-committing-to-wasting-time/

Mantel, Hilary, 'Can These Bones Live?', *The Reith Lectures*, Radio 4, 2017 https://www.bbc.co.uk/programmes/b08wp3g3

——, in interview with Alex Clark, *Guardian*, 22 February 2020 https://www.theguardian.com/books/2020/feb/22/hilary-mantel-ive-got-quite-amused-at-people-saying-i-have-writers-block-ive-been-like-a-factory

Marsh, Kate (ed.), *Writers and Their Houses: A Guide to the Writers' Houses of England, Scotland, Wales and Ireland* (London: Hamish Hamilton, 1993)

Marshall, Paule, 'Poets in the Kitchen', *Callaloo*, 24, No. 2 (spring 2001), pp. 627–33

Masud, Noreen, 'Shelf Life', *Lunate*, 8 August 2024, https://www.lunate.co.uk/features/noreen-masuds-shelf-life

Micciche, Laura R., 'Writers have always loved mobile devices', *The Atlantic*, 18 August 2018, https://www.theatlantic.com/technology/archive/2018/08/writers-have-always-loved-mobile-devices/567637/

Miller, Edward, 'Antonio Panizzi and the British Museum', *The British Library Journal*, Vol. 5, No. 1 (1979)

Moraga, Cherríe L., and Gloria E. Anzaldúa (eds), *This Bridge Called My Back* (Berkeley: Third Woman Press, 2002)

Oates, Joyce Carol, @JoyceCarolOates, Twitter/X, 16 March 2021, 4.23, https://x.com/JoyceCarolOates/status/1371859718650597387?lang=en

O'Connor, Eva, personal correspondence, 21 September 2024

Olsen, Porter, 'Emulation as Mimicry: Reading the Salman Rushdie Digital Archive', *South Asian Review*, Vol. 40, No. 3 (2019)

Olsen, Tillie, *Silences* (London: Virago, 1979)

Orwell, George, *Keep the Aspidistra Flying* (London: Penguin, 1989)

Oyler, Lauren, 'The Thou of Zadie Smith', *Baffler*, 6 February 2018, https://thebaffler.com/latest/the-thou-of-zadie-smith-oyler

Pankejeff, Sergei, 'My recollections of Sigmund Freud', in M. Gardiner (ed.), *The Wolf-Man and Sigmund Freud* (New York: Basic Books, 1971) pp. 135–52

Pettegree, Andrew, and Arthur der Weduwen, *Library: A Fragile History* (London: Profile, 2021)

Phillips, Caryl, 'A house is not a home', *Times Literary Supplement*, 6 December 2024, https://www.the-tls.co.uk/lives/biography/the-importance-of-place-to-james-baldwin-essay-caryl-phillips

Potter, Dennis, *The Singing Detective*, directed by Jon Amiel, BBC, 1986

Pritchard, Alli, Monk's House manager, personal correspondence, 19 October 2022.

Ravn, Olga, *My Work*, trans. Sophia Hersi Smith and Jennifer Russell (London: Lolli, 2023)

'Reading for Pleasure', *National Literacy Trust*, https://literacytrust.org.uk/reading-for-pleasure/

Roach, Rebecca, '"Do You Use a Pencil or a Pen?": Author Interviews as Literary Advice', in Anneleen Masschelein and Dirk de Geest (eds), *Writing Manuals for the Masses. New Directions in Book History* (London: Palgrave Macmillan, 2021), p. 345

Rooney, Sally, in interview with Róisín Ingle, *Irish Times*, 4 September 2021, https://www.irishtimes.com/culture/books/sally-rooney-i-m-really-paranoid-about-my-personal-life-i-feel-self-conscious-1.4655068`

——, in interview with Martin Doyle, *Irish Times*, 24 September 2024, https://www.irishtimes.com/culture/books/2024/09/14/sally-rooney-there-is-something-christian-about-my-work-even-if-i-would-not-describe-myself-as-religious/

——, 'Loving the Limitations of the Novel: A Conversation between Sally Rooney and Merve Emre', *The Paris Review*, 9 October 2024, https://www.theparisreview.org/blog/2024/10/09/loving-the-limitations-of-thenovel-a-conversation-between-sally-rooney-and-merve-emre/

Rosner, Victoria, *Machines for Living* (Oxford: Oxford University Press, 2020)

Rothfeld, Becca, 'Normal Novels', *The Point*, 28 January 2020, https://thepointmag.com/criticism/normal-novels/

Ruefle, Mary, *Madness, Rack, and Honey* (Seattle: Wave Books, 2012)

Scanlon, Kath, Fanny Blanc, Annie Edge and Christine Whitehead, 'The Bank of Mum and Dad: How it *Really* Works', LSE Report for Family Building Society, January 2019, https://www.lse.ac.uk/business/consulting/assets/documents/the-bank-of-mum-and-dad.pdf

Schwartz, Alexandra, 'Sheila Heti wrestles with a big decision in "Motherhood"', *The New Yorker*, 30 April 2018, https://www.newyorker.com/magazine/2018/05/07/sheila-heti-wrestles-with-a-big-decision-in-motherhood

Press release, 'At least 354,000 people homeless in England today', Shelter, 11 December 2024, https://england.shelter.org.uk/media/press_release/at_least_354000_people_homeless_in_england_today_

Smith, Ali, 'The Art of Fiction no. 236', interview by Adam Begley, *The Paris Review*, Issue 221 (summer 2017), https://www.theparisreview.org/interviews/6949/the-art-of-fiction-no-236-ali-smith

Smith, Barbara, 'A Press of Our Own Kitchen Table: Women of Color Press', *Frontiers: A Journal of Women's Studies*, Vol. 10, No. 3 (1989), pp. 11–13

Smith, Zadie, in conversation with Christopher Bollen, *Interview*, 24 August 2012, https://www.interviewmagazine.com/culture/zadie-smith

——, on Charlie Rose, YouTube, uploaded by Remembrance of Things Past, 27 March 2020, https://www.youtube.com/watch?v=5IS6W1dnSec

Swinton, Tilda, 'Residences', *Prospect Cottage – Creative Folkestone*, January 2020, https://www.creativefolkestone.org.uk/prospect-cottage/residencies/

Tate, Claudia, *Black Women Writers at Work* (Chicago: Haymarket Books, 1983)

Thomas, Amy, Michele Battisti and Martin Kretschmer, 'UK Authors' Earning and Contracts 2022: A Survey of 60,000 Writers', CreatE, University of Glasgow

Time magazine, 12 April 1937, https://content.time.com/time/covers/0,16641,19370412,00.html

Editorial, *Time* magazine, 12 April 1937, https://time.com/archive/6778966/books-how-time-passes/

Townsend, Sue, *The Secret Diary of Adrian Mole Aged 13 ¾* (London: Methuen, 1983)

Waal, Kit de, 'Make room for working class writers', *Guardian*, 10 February 2018, https://www.theguardian.com/books/2018/feb/10/kit-de-waal-where-are-all-the-working-class-writers-

Walker, Alice, *In Search of Our Mother's Gardens* (London: Phoenix Books, 2005)

Watson, Nicola J., *The Author's Effects: On Writer's House Museums* (Oxford: Oxford University Press, 2020)

Watt, Ian, *Rise of the Novel* (London: Penguin, 1966)

Webb, Ralf, personal correspondence, 27 January 2025

Welland, Freydis Jane, 'The History of Jane Austen's Writing Desk', *Persuasions*, 20 (2008)

Weller, Christian E., and Lily Roberts, 'Eliminating the Black-White Wealth Gap is a Generational Challenge', *American Progress*, 19 March 2021, https://www.americanprogress.org/article/eliminating-black-white-wealth-gap-generational-challenge/

Williams, Raymond, *Drama in Performance* (London: Frederick Muller, 1954)

Woolf, Leonard, *Downhill All the Way: An Autobiography of the Years 1919–1939* (London: Hogarth Press, 1967)

Woolf, Virginia (unsigned), 'Haworth, November 1904', *Guardian*, 21 December 1904

——, *A Room of One's Own* [1929] (London: Penguin, 1973)

——, *The London Scene* [1931] (London: Daunt, 2013)

——, 'The Leaning Tower', *The Moment and Other Essays* (London: Hogarth Press, 1947)

——, *The Diary of Virginia Woolf*, Volume 1: *1915–1919*, edited by Anne Oliver Bell (London: Penguin, 1979)

——, *The Diary of Virginia Woolf*, Volume 3: *1925–1930*, edited by Anne Oliver Bell and Andre McNeillie (London: Harcourt Brace Jovanovich, 1980)

Young, Iris Marion, 'House and Home: Feminist Variations on a Theme', in *On Female Body Experience: 'Throwing Like a Girl' and Other Essays* (Oxford: Oxford University, 2006)

Young, Melissa, 'How to Look Like a Writer', WikiHow, https://www.wikihow.com/Look-Like-a-Writer

Zaborowska, Magdalena J., *James Baldwin's Turkish Decade* (London, Duke University Press: 2008)

——, *Me and My House* (London: Duke University Press, 2018)

INDEX

A
Adaptation (2002 film) 87–8
AI platforms 183–4, 202
All About Eve (1950 film) 85
Allingham, Helen 53
Alton, Hampshire 191
Angelou, Maya 168–9, 216
Anzaldúa, Gloria E. 150–1
Austen, Jane 65, 171, 172, 191
Austen-Leigh, James Edward 171–2

B
Baldwin, James 124–5, 161–3, 186, 188–91
  'Chez Baldwin' 186, 188–91
  Go Tell It on the Mountain 124–5, 163
  The Welcome Table 188
Ballard, Bea 132–3
Ballard, J. G. 132–3
Balzac, Honoré de 41
  La Comédie humaine 41
Barnes, Julian 15–16, 93
  Flaubert's Parrot 15–16
Barthes, Roland 73, 128
Baudelaire, Charles 163–4
Beauvoir, Simone de 127–8
  The Second Sex 127

Behn, Aphra 130
bell hooks 212–13
Bell, Vanessa 30, 36, 37
Benjamin, Walter 163–5
Bishop, Liam 159–60
Bolbec Hall, Newcastle 201
Bonaparte, Princess Marie 48
Bougie London Literary Woman 101–3
Bourdieu, Pierre 102
British Library 110–13, 119–20, 122–3, 150, 160
British Museum 23, 120–3
  Reading Room 23, 120–1
British Museum Act (1753) 120
Brodkey, Linda 8–9
Brontë family 32–3, 108, 138–40, 172
Buckley, William F. 97

C
Café de Flore, Paris 163
cafes 148, 153–60, 163–4
Calleja, Jen 20–1
Cameron, David 103–4
Capote, Truman 174
Carlyle, Jane 51, 54
Carlyle, Thomas 32, 51–7

241

INDEX

Carlyle's House 51–7, 58
Carlyle's House Memorial Trust 51–2, 58
Catton, Eleanor 95
Cavendish, Margaret 129
Charles Dickens Museum 12–13, 57–8, 169–71
chatbots 183–4
Chester, Eliza Jane 60
Christie, Agatha 40, 166–8
    Greenway House 167
    Pera Palace Hotel, Istanbul 167–8
Chu, Andrea Long 81
Clark, Eliza 95
Clifton, Fred 195
Clifton House, Baltimore, Maryland 195–6, 200
Clifton, Lucille 64, 65, 195
Coel, Michaela 89–90
collaboration, writing in 144–7, 201
Collins, Keith 198
computers 177, 180–2
Connolly, Cyril 24
Connor, Steven 63
Cooper, Emily 98–9
Covid-19 pandemic 21–2
Crewe, Tom 93–4, 95
Cusk, Rachel 128

D
Dahl, Roald 62–3
Davidson, Sophie 95–6
Davis, Bette 85
Davis, Thadious M. 193
DeLillo, Don 10, 73–4
    Mao II 10
Derrida, Jacques 180–1
Dickens, Charles 12–13, 57–8, 169–170, 214
    Charles Dickens Museum 12–13, 57–8, 169–71
    Dickens's Dream (Buss) 214
    travel desk 169–70
Dickinson, Emily 42–4, 129, 151
    Emily Dickinson Museum 43–4
Didion, Joan 68, 69–71, 107, 183
Dillon, Brian 97–8, 178
    I Am Sitting in a Room 97–8
Doolittle, Hilda (H.D.) 47
Drabble, Margaret, *The Millstone* 129
Duras, Marguerite 209–10
Dürer, Albrecht 5
Dyer, Geoff 91–2

E
Elkin, Lauren 20, 178–9
    No. 91/92: notes on a Parisian commute 178–9
Emecheta, Buchi, *Second Class Citizen* 147
Engelman, Edmund 48

F
fatherhood, writing and 132–3, 134
feminist writing 25, 126–37
Ferrante, Elena 83–4
films, writers in 14, 86–90
Franzen, Jonathan 99–100
Freud Museum London 13, 45, 46–7, 48–50
Freud, Sigmund 13, 45–50
    therapeutic couch 45–6, 63–4
    writing desk 45, 46, 49

G
Gaskell, Elizabeth, *The Life of Charlotte Brontë* 32, 139
Gay, Roxane 77
Gerrey, Alta 130–1, 133–4
Ghansah, Rachel Kaadzi 189–90
Gilman, Charlotte Perkins, *The Yellow Wallpaper* 126–7

INDEX

Goddard, Keiran 179
Granta magazine 93–5
Greene, Justin Russell 99

H

Haigney, Sophie 69
Hamilton, Alexander 171
Hamilton, Patrick, *Monday Morning* 7–8
Hanks, Tom, *Uncommon Type* 176
Hardwick, Elizabeth 51
Haussmann, Georges-Eugène 164
Hemingway, Ernest 155–7, 183
   A Moveable Feast 155–7
Hill, Rosemary 100
hipsters 175–6
Historic Joy Kogawa House 196–7
Hoberman, Ruth 121–2
Hogarth Press 37
Hogarth, William *x*, 10–11
Hollywood films 14, 84–9
homelessness 116
Honoré de Balzac House, Paris 41
hotel rooms 167–9
Hucks, London 148
Hugo, Victor 65–6
Hurston, Zora Neale 193–4

I

I May Destroy You (2020 TV series) 89–90
Idler magazine 76
In a Lonely Place (1950 film) 86

J

James, Selma 152–3
Jarman, Derek 197–9
   Prospect Cottage 197–9
Jerome, St 5–6
Johnson, Georgia Douglas 192–3

K

Kapil, Bhanu 211–12
Kaufman, Charlie 87–8
Keats House 59–62, 73, 106–7
Keats, John 59–62, 64, 73, 106–7
Kerouac, Jack 174, 199
   On the Road 174
Kerr, Judith 134–6
Kitchen Table: Women of Color Press 136–7
Kogawa, Joy 196–7
Kureishi, Carlo 144–5
Kureishi, Hanif 143–5

L

Lafarge, Daisy 118–19
Lawley, Sue 72–3
Le Guin, Ursula 136
Lee, Hermione 13
Leilani, Raven, *Luster* 105–6
Levy, Deborah, *The Cost of Living* 165–6
libraries 119, 124–5
   see also British Library; New York Public Library
lodge, writing 28, 36, 37, 104, 150
London Writers' Salon 145–6
Lorde, Audre 136, 151–2
Lorentzen, Christian 78
Lumsden, George A. 51–2, 53
Lyons, Martyn 172–3

M

Ma, Ling 185
Magee, Michael 118
Mantel, Hilary 72–3, 91
Marshall, Paule 137–8
Masud, Noreen 179
Medland, Amber 147, 180
Micciche, Laura R. 171
millennial writers 105–6

243

INDEX

Monk's House 28, 29–31, 33–42, 58–9, 74–5
Montagu House 120
Morris, William 107, 191
motherhood, writing and 125–9, 131, 136, 142–3, 147, 209
   Mothers Who Write network 145
Murder She Wrote (US TV series) 174, 177
Murray, Simone 77–8

N

National Centre for Children's Books 135–6
Navarro, Brenda 92
Nazi Germany 47–8
New York Public Library 124–5
New York Times 72, 159

O

Oates, Joyce Carol 77, 78
O'Connor, Eva 160
Olsen, Tillie 129, 131, 151, 205
Opportunity magazine 193
Orwell, George, *Keep the Aspidistra Flying* 9, 114–6
Oyler, Lauren 80

P

Panizzi, Antonio 121–2
Pankejeff, Sergei (The Wolf Man) 45–6
Parker, Cornelia, *Exhaled Blanket* 63
Pera Palace Hotel, Istanbul 167–8
Perec, Georges 95
Phillips, Caryl 189
Pollan, Michael 104
popular culture, writers in 14, 83, 89–90, 159
portraits, author 30–1, 74, 76, 83, 93–100, 214

Potter, Dennis 140–1
Prospect Cottage 197–9
Proust, Marcel 15
Pynchon, Thomas 83

R

Ravn, Olga, *My Work* 215
Ray, Nicholas, *In a Lonely Place* 86
Roach, Rebecca 70
Roald Dahl Museum and Story Centre, Great Missenden 62–3
Rooney, Sally 14, 81–3, 106, 182
   Intermezzo 81
Rosler, Martha, *Semiotics of the Kitchen* 128
Rosner, Victoria 36
Rothfeld, Becca 106
Ruefle, Mary 44
Rushdie, Salman 181

S

Salinger, J. D. 83
Schiller, Rebecca 145
Schwartz, Alexandra 126
Shakespeare in Love (1998 film) 88–9
Shakespeare, Wiliam 75, 88–9, 97
Shange, Ntozake 159
sheds, writing 9, 36, 38, 62–3, 104, 165–6
Singing Detective, The (1986 BBC drama) 140–2
Sitwell, Edith 119
Smith, Ali 105
Smith, Barbara 136–7
Smith, Zadie 79–81, 95
   Feel Free 80
   Intimations 80–1
   White Teeth 79
social media 70, 77, 78, 101–3
solitude, writer's 10, 23–4, 66–7, 75, 209–10, 212–13

INDEX

Sontag, Susan 95, 98
Spark, Muriel 114
Stephen, Caroline Amelia 206
Stephen, Sir Leslie 52
Strachey, Lytton 41–2
Strand magazine 75–6
Substack 143–4
Swinton, Tilda 199

T

Tait, Robert 53
technology 177–184
teenage writing rooms 3, 6
Thomas, Dylan 104
Time magazine 74
tourism, literary 12, 45, 75, 123
Townsend, Sue, *The Secret Diary of Adrian Mole Aged 13 ¾* 6–7
Trumbo, Dalton 15
Twain, Mark 199
Twitter/X 70, 77, 101–3
typewriters 4, 26, 172–6
    Agatha Christie and 40, 167
    Susan Sontag and 95, 98

U

'unmasking' writers 83–4

V

virtual tours 43, 64–6

W

Waal, Kit de 117
Walker, Alice 193–4
Watson, Nicola J. 12, 39–40, 62
Watt, Ian, *The Rise of the Novel* 130
Webb, Ralf 210–11

Welland, Freydis Jane 171
West-Knights, Imogen 101–3
Wharton, Edith 40–1, 199
    The Mount 41
William Morris Gallery 107, 191
Williams, Raymond 208–9
Winfrey, Oprah 99
Winterson, Jeanette 36, 37–8
Woolf, Leonard
    at Monk's House 29, 34, 36, 37
    on Virginia's writing set up 38–9, 40, 41–42
Woolf, Virginia 14–5, 23–4, 25, 28, 29–40, 54–7, 74–5, 104, 120–1, 129, 130, 150, 168, 206–8, 217
    Monk's House 28, 29–30, 31, 33–42, 58–9, 74–5
    portraits 30–1, 74
    writing desk 28, 37
    writing lodge 28, 36, 37, 150
    'Great Men's Houses' 54–7
    Orlando 30
    A Room of One's Own 23–4, 120–1, 129, 206–8, 217
    Three Guineas 207
    To the Lighthouse 30
writer's block, 86–88, 91–2, 99–101, 106, 140, 215

Y

Young, Iris Marion 134

Z

Zambreno, Kate 147
Zola, Emile 76
Zoo, Alice 93–5